WILLIE APIATA, VC

WILLIE APIATA
—VC—

THE RELUCTANT HERO

PAUL LITTLE

VIKING

VIKING

Published by the Penguin Group
Penguin Group (NZ), 67 Apollo Drive, Rosedale,
North Shore 0632, New Zealand (a division of Pearson New Zealand Ltd)
Penguin Group (USA) Inc., 375 Hudson Street,
New York, New York 10014, USA
Penguin Group (Canada), 90 Eglinton Avenue East, Suite 700, Toronto,
Ontario, M4P 2Y3, Canada (a division of Pearson Penguin Canada Inc.)
Penguin Books Ltd, 80 Strand, London, WC2R 0RL, England
Penguin Ireland, 25 St Stephen's Green,
Dublin 2, Ireland (a division of Penguin Books Ltd)
Penguin Group (Australia), 250 Camberwell Road, Camberwell,
Victoria 3124, Australia (a division of Pearson Australia Group Pty Ltd)
Penguin Books India Pvt Ltd, 11, Community Centre,
Panchsheel Park, New Delhi – 110 017, India
Penguin Books (South Africa) (Pty) Ltd, 24 Sturdee Avenue,
Rosebank, Johannesburg 2196, South Africa

Penguin Books Ltd, Registered Offices: 80 Strand, London, WC2R 0RL, England

First published in 2008
1 3 5 7 9 10 8 6 4 2

Designed and typeset by Pindar (NZ)
Printed in Australia by McPherson's Printing Group

ISBN 978 0 670073 20 7

A catalogue record for this book is available
from the National Library of New Zealand.

www.penguin.co.nz

All images courtesy of the Apiata family except the following:
Dave Woods: Insert 1 page 8 (below)
1NZSAS: Insert 2 pages 3, 4 (above), 5, 6 (above), 7 (above);
insert 3 pages 3, 6 (above), 7, 8
NZDF: Insert 2 pages 7 (below), 8; insert 3 pages 1, 2, 6 (below)
Willy Sussman: Insert 3 pages 3 (below), 4
Palmerston North Boys' High School: Insert 3 page 5 (above)

But who are ye, in rags and rotten shoes,
You dirty bearded, blocking up the way?
We are the Pilgrims, master; we shall go
Always a little further; it may be
Beyond the last blue mountain barred with snow
Across that angry glimmering sea.

James Elroy Flecker
The Golden Journey to Samarkand

Who Dares Wins

FOREWORD

On Monday, 2 July 2007 I had the great privilege of informing the members of the 1st New Zealand Special Air Service Group (via a pre-recorded video announcement) that four of their comrades were to be recognised for their actions in Afghanistan in 2004.

Two individuals in 1 NZSAS Group were to be awarded the New Zealand Gallantry Decoration (NZGD) for acts of exceptional gallantry in situations of danger. Another would receive the New Zealand Gallantry Medal (NZGM) for his act of bravery. These actions occurred over several incidents and these men, in normal NZSAS fashion, were to receive no public attention.

The final announcement was that Her Majesty the Queen had bestowed the Victoria Cross (VC) for New Zealand on Corporal Willie Apiata. Corporal Apiata, VC, and I were already in Wellington as I had informed him of his award the day before.

Corporal Apiata, VC, was to be the first ever recipient of the Victoria Cross for New Zealand since it was instituted in 1999 as part of the shift to the New Zealand honours system from the previous British awards process.

Since its inception in 1856 just 21 New Zealanders have won the VC, with Charles Upham also being the only combatant to ever receive a second (or bar) for his actions in the Second World War. Corporal Apiata, VC, is only the 14th recipient, and the first New Zealander, to be awarded the medal since the end of the Second World War.

To put his achievement in perspective, the VC is officially awarded for 'most conspicuous gallantry, or some daring or pre-eminent act of valour, self-sacrifice or extreme devotion to duty in the presence of the enemy', an act for which the chance of survival is presumed to be as low as 10 per cent.

Prior to the announcement I had considered for some time the ramifications this award would have for Corporal Apiata and 1 NZSAS Group. We would have to allow the door to our discreet world to open ever so slightly and expose one of our members to the media spotlight – his world would never be the same again. This did not sit comfortably with me, nor would it with Corporal Apiata and the unit. It is simply not part of our culture to speak of our deeds or operations. We prefer to go about our business in the traditional way we have since 1955 – with little fuss and no need for accolades.

I am not surprised, and am indeed proud, that every member of the NZSAS Group has provided support, encouragement and comradeship to help sustain Corporal Apiata, VC, through the past 14 months since his public life began.

This public exposure has called on even more resolve from Corporal Apiata, VC, to perform duties never expected of any serving soldier, let alone a humble Kiwi boy from Te Kaha. And he has performed these to the required minimum standard of the SAS – with excellence.

This book has been written to serve as an explanation and further introduction to the man who has become New Zealand's newest hero. It tells the story of an ordinary Kiwi, proud of his country and with a deep love of family, his fellow soldiers and heritage, who, when faced with an incredible set of circumstances, put the safety and survival of his mates above all else and performed acts of gallantry that will stand forever in this country's history.

Truthfully, Corporal Apiata, VC, would have preferred to never have been acknowledged publicly. When I informed him of his award on the morning of 1 July 2007 his first words to me were to ask if his wounded friend Cpl 'D' knew. He then told me that he was 'just doing his job' and followed by saying, 'You're going to out me, aren't you, boss?' Corporal Apiata, VC, quickly reached the same conclusion I had – non disclosure was just not an option. As a result, the public's appetite and demand for his time have been, at times, insatiable. It was therefore decided to use this medium to tell his story. Hopefully, Corporal Apiata, VC, can now go about his life again – doing what he does best and loves for as long as he wishes to – continuing to serve his country as an active member of the NZSAS Group.

As if those acts on the battlefield were not enough, Corporal Apiata, VC, has since proven capable of even greater deeds. His subsequent gifting of his Victoria Cross to the NZSAS Trust, and therefore the people of New Zealand, is a mark of the respect he has for those he serves with and those who were alongside him that day. Had I allowed him to do so, he would have wandered into his Squadron's hangar in his normal unassuming way, had a few quiet words with the boys to let them know, and that would have been the end of it. That would simply not have been right.

Since this announcement the NZSAS has been publicly exposed as never before; however, throughout it all we remain a strong, unified and proud unit, singularly focused and on our never-ending journey on the road to serve with excellence.

In general, the media have treated Willie and the NZSAS with the dignity and respect we requested. I would like to thank them for that. For the small minority who did not, they are entitled to exercise their right to freedom of speech, that very right that we soldiers serve to protect.

As the Commanding Officer of 1 NZSAS Group, I am immensely proud and privileged to serve alongside these soldiers who daily, to a person, perform beyond expectations and put the success of their task or mission ahead of themselves. This country can be proud that the New Zealand Defence Force has been, and will always continue to be, fully prepared to serve New Zealand wherever and whenever required with distinction.

September 2008
Commanding Officer
1 NZSAS Group

CONTENTS

PROLOGUE   THE SANCTUARY   15

CHAPTER ONE   THE BIG BACKYARD   19

CHAPTER TWO   HUNTER   34

CHAPTER THREE   THRILL SEEKER   43

CHAPTER FOUR   ROAD WARRIOR   50

CHAPTER FIVE   SOLDIER   66

CHAPTER SIX   FISHERMAN   80

CHAPTER SEVEN   TRAVELLER   87

CHAPTER EIGHT   PEACEKEEPER   98

CHAPTER NINE   INSIDER   107

CHAPTER TEN   FAST LEARNER   121

CHAPTER ELEVEN   INITIATE   138

CHAPTER TWELVE   BADGED MEMBER   144

CHAPTER THIRTEEN   GOOD SOLDIER   155

CHAPTER FOURTEEN   MENTOR IN TRAINING   168

CHAPTER FIFTEEN   WILLIE APIATA, VC   182

CHAPTER SIXTEEN   CELEBRITY   192

CHAPTER SEVENTEEN   RELUCTANT HERO   202

CHAPTER EIGHTEEN	TE KAHA	209
CHAPTER NINETEEN	EUROPE	218
CHAPTER TWENTY	PAPAKURA	228
CHAPTER TWENTY-ONE	WAITANGI	237
AFTERWORD	THE TEST	251
APPENDIX	NEW ZEALAND VICTORIA CROSS WINNERS	253

'People are calling you a hero. Are you a hero?'

'I'm Willie Apiata.'

PROLOGUE

THE SANCTUARY

Papakura, south of Auckland, has been home to a military base since 1940. Today it is also the site of Rennie Lines, built 50 years later as the headquarters of the 1st New Zealand Special Air Service Group.

Rennie Lines is both hidden and not hidden. If you know where to look, it is impossible to miss. If you don't know where to look, it is impossible to see. The heart of the complex is a nondescript collection of large, white utilitarian sheds, all surrounded by a high fence which is electrified. These contain the facilities for the day-to-day operations of the SAS.

Visitors are not encouraged. A heavy automatic gate moves slowly to let them in and out, and personnel's impatience is barely concealed while they wait for it to close, as they always must, when entering or leaving.

Inside Group Headquarters are a reception area and meeting rooms downstairs and offices upstairs. Members of the unit seldom ascend past the lower level. When a soldier is summoned higher, to see the Commanding Officer, it is because he is either in trouble or about to be given a task. The news may not be bad, but it will most probably be challenging.

The lower-level rooms reflect the SAS's keen awareness of its traditions. The History Room contains a small library heavy on military memoirs, thrillers, books on weapons and a comprehensive set of travel guides. It is lined with displays depicting past New Zealand SAS operations – from its first, in Malaya in 1955, through Thailand, Borneo, Vietnam, Bougainville, Kuwait and East Timor to Afghanistan in 2002. There is no record of more recent operations.

The reception area is dominated by a large carving depicting the ethos of the SAS, as well as some of its activities. At its centre is a scout covering a tracker who is studying a footprint. Within the footprint is a likeness of the SAS's founder, David Stirling. At the base is a waka taua – war canoe – symbolising the journey an SAS soldier takes during his training. In front of the carving is a large piece of lapis lazuli, acquired in Afghanistan.

Also in the foyer, a glass-walled trophy room bulges with photos, plaques, cups, weapons and other memorabilia. Tucked away in a corner next to the carving is a small glass case containing a Victoria Cross. It is neither spotlit nor raised on a podium like the Holy Grail. It takes its place alongside other items representing the traditions of the unit.

In the grounds outside the electrified walls lies a chapel, a historic building removed from its original location at another defence facility. There are also a war memorial and a tribute to the Long Range Desert Group, the proto-guerrillas of the Second World War whose members, half of them New Zealanders, played a significant part in the early operations of Stirling's original SAS.

A well-appointed mess serves up carbohydrate-heavy meals, in a dining room adjacent to which is the Hunting Lodge – a gentlemen's club-type extravaganza of schist walls, giant fireplaces and a menagerie's worth of mounted game animal heads, from moose to boar, a captured Nazi flag and other souvenirs. In one part of the bar, the front half of a Long Range Desert Group jeep protrudes from the wall, and there is also a life-sized photo of the prototypical reluctant hero, Sir Edmund Hillary, with his larger than life-size autograph.

Beyond that are the barracks, named for the various NZSAS campaigns. Outside one of these may be parked a gleaming black monster of a ute. Its owner's room contains a single man's basics – bed, couches, fridge, toaster, TV set and DVD player – as well as photos of family members from across the generations. A bottle of SAS port and a can of CRC sit alongside snapshots of his son. But there are also numerous unique souvenirs. A Wilkinson sword from a market in Afghanistan will one day be worked into a knife to be used on pig-hunting expeditions in the Bay of Plenty. Pinned to a wall is the silhouette of a human figure, peppered with bullet holes after being used for target practice with a recently acquired machine gun. The grouping of the shots is impressive. An awe-inspiring, intricately carved tokotoko – walking stick or staff – showing his whakapapa, marvellous in its workmanship, has been given to its owner only recently. The hide of the first deer he killed serves as a floor rug.

There is also a set of medals in replica. To other members of the SAS, the room's occupant is a comrade, someone they work alongside. With them he can enjoy a dose of anonymity that is precious now, for outside these walls, to the rest of New Zealand and the world, he is not just a corporal in the SAS. He is Willie Apiata, holder of the first Victoria Cross for New Zealand. Rennie Lines is the perfect sanctuary for this reluctant hero.

CHAPTER ONE

THE BIG BACKYARD

Whatever the exact combination of qualities that saw Willie Apiata perform the deeds that earned him the Victoria Cross, there is no doubt many of them were acquired in the course of a rural New Zealand childhood that was by turns exhilarating and arduous, inspiring and idyllic. Resourcefulness, self-reliance, personal courage, loyalty, hard work, stamina – all these attributes run deep in both Willie and his family.

Although he wasn't especially aware of it while he was growing up, there is a military tradition in his background. His mother's father, Jim, fought and was a POW in the Second World War. Like many survivors of that conflict, Jim seldom talked about his war service, but there are photographs. Willie's paternal grandfather also served in the Second World War, but Willie does not know any details of his service. And his father's brother fought in Vietnam.

Accompanying this military orientation is a family culture of hard work. Jim was a fencer famous for his sheer physical strength and awe-inspiring stamina – traits he passed on to his daughter, who used to work alongside him even as a child, and to his grandchildren. He respected hard work and a healthy appetite. Working around Mangakino and Turangi, where fences he made still stand on the area's farms, he would continue well into the night, marking out the roughest of country by the light of kerosene-tin lamps. Where today explosives would be used to break through rock, Jim would chip relentlessly away at the stone with a crowbar until it was reduced to rubble. He and his dog would sleep where he stopped, their accommodation a large corrugated-iron tank with a wire strapped over the top and pegged into the ground so it wouldn't roll away.

Later, when Willie's mum and her brother, Harry, went with Jim they would sit in the tank, warming themselves beside a kerosene tin full of hot embers for a heater, while their father continued to work outside, indifferent to bitter winter snows. When they went with him, the children would help. After Jim cut and peeled posts the right size, the children would strip the smaller branches off them and the posts were then chopped by hand, and piled up for trucks to collect.

An equally strong tradition in Willie's family is the ability to source food from the land. In the winter of 2006, when he took his mother to Ohakune, where her own mother, Phyllis, who died young, is buried, Willie's mum showed him the stream where she used to catch trout, flipping them out of the water and into the pan – the only way to eat the fish, she told him.

When Willie was two years old, his mother had a clairvoyant reading done on her son. It predicted that he would be either the master of a ship or an army commander. She only told her son about this prophecy when he joined the Army nearly two decades later.

Willie's mother is Pakeha. His father is Maori, of Nga Puhi descent. In their early years together, the pair worked around the once numerous small-town mills where native timber was processed. Willie would play in the dirt while the work went on around him and the ancient trucks, more often than not bereft of doors or bonnet, pulled up to deliver native logs.

At other times, his parents would find employment on farms. As a farm hand, his father worked with dry stock, doing everything from mustering to managing animals and maintaining farms as well as fencing and shearing. It was while working at a native mill in Mangakino in 1972 that he became the father of Bill Henry Apiata, their third child after two daughters. Another daughter would come later. Because more than one of the children was born around the same time of year, for many years the pragmatic and thrifty mother celebrated their birthdays jointly, on June 15, creating some confusion among her offspring about who was actually born when. Willie only found out much later, when completing some paperwork for which he needed his birth certificate, that he was born on June 28. He was named Bill after a family friend, Henry after his mum's father.

True to form and family, Willie's mum worked hard right through her pregnancies and afterwards. Although money was tight, and the walls of the house were lined with newspaper rather than wallpaper, the family home was kept spotless. Farm jobs meant she could take her children with her to work from an early age, which she liked.

The family moved from small town to small town, depending on where the work was. Living in or near native bush, they often fed on what they had hunted. Willie's parents would pack up the children and head into the bush, driving as far as they could and walking the rest of the way with their offspring in tow. Occasionally there would be huts to sleep in, but if not they camped out in their sleeping bags. They only went when the weather was warm, and they didn't bother with tents. A tarpaulin might be taken along for emergencies. In this way, work and play, finding food and learning how to live were all bound together in the children's daily lives. They had the biggest backyard imaginable – the bush – which was their playground as well as their pantry.

Slipping away from their parents, Willie and his sisters would head into the bush and be gone for hours, making huts and playing hide-and-seek or the game they called 'water rats', which involved walking along creeks to catch eels and frogs by blind spearing – stabbing a spike into the water and throwing anything unlucky enough to get caught on the end of it off to one side.

One interest of Willie's that the girls didn't share was his beloved toy soldiers. He had plastic bread bags full of little men with machine guns and bazookas. He and his friends spent hours mounting imaginary battles. Once, they armed themselves with picks and shovels and created a command post for themselves and their diminutive troops by digging up a farmer's field and making a hill around which they arranged the soldiers. The farmer was furious when he caught them. The boys ran for it, but Willie's uncle made them go back, apologise and fill in the holes they had made.

Eventually, when Willie was seven years old, his parents split up. She and the children stayed briefly in Salvation Army accommodation in Whangarei, but she had been to Te Kaha on a visit and liked it, and it was to this small East Coast town, one of New Zealand's loveliest and least populated, that she moved with her children. Willie would come to regard Awakoko at Te Kaha as home. It would be many years before he returned north.

His mum never found another man to settle down with permanently. As she sees it, she chose her children over a partner, and she didn't want to burden them with another father figure. It was a decision she never regretted. If it made life harder and lonelier, and bred trials and tribulations – well, she was used to all that. Others saw her for the good mother she was, and she became one of those women who end up taking care of other people's children and their problems as well as her own. Bullied and beaten strays would end up at his mum's house. However, she drew the line at official fostering, despite requests from social workers.

Going off on your own with four children is sufficient challenge for any woman, even one as hardy as Willie's mum. It was often lonely, especially when decisions had to be made about what the children needed or how to handle the day-to-day choices any parent must make. There was no sounding board, no second opinion. But the shared adversity brought mother and children close together as a tight five whose bond is as solid as tempered steel.

Willie didn't receive any special treatment or regard because he was the only boy in his family. To his mum, all her children were special. To their credit, the girls probably didn't dress him up in skirts and high heels or make him play with their dolls any more than most boys with three sisters have to endure. When he was very little he simply wanted to be around his sisters and do what they did. If that meant being used as a dress-up doll, that was fine. Teasing never went much further than the traditional 'close your eyes and I'll give you a big surprise' before taking a barefoot sibling for a walk into a cowpat.

Willie's mum worked hard just to keep her children fed and clothed. Entertainment had to be free – there simply wasn't the money for lots of toys and treats. A bike was a prized possession and his mum struggled to get her children bikes long after their friends had them. The time Willie's golden three-wheeler was run over and damaged is still talked about.

One advantage to their way of life, from the children's point of view, was that they were left to their own devices more than they otherwise might have been. Willie and his sisters were raised to be strong, fit and capable. They had to be. With so much space to roam around in, it was impossible for their mum to always keep them within earshot. So they were taught to fend for themselves from an early age. Despite what would be seen as a high-risk lifestyle requiring knee pads and helmets today, injuries were few.

They were shown how to cope with any new situation or environment before being left to handle it on their own. As soon as they were old enough, they were taught to swim. A river was a challenge to be swum across or swung over on vines, although even his mum's liberal parenting style was stretched on the day she looked out her window to see a river in flood – and her children thundering down it on logs. Similarly, if she had told the children once, she had told them a hundred times not to go near the beehives by the house. But clad in singlet and shorts and bearing sticks they set out to do battle with the hives, and were appropriately set upon as a result. On another notable occasion young Willie was stung by a bumblebee that flew up his shorts.

One dry summer's day, the young gang decided to deal to a small umbrella wasps' nest in a tree next to their house. Drawing on reserves of initiative and foolhardiness in equal measure, Willie's solution involved petrol and matches. He got a piece of hose and sucked some fuel from a petrol tank. Then he gave his youngest sister some matches. While he sprayed the nest, she threw a lit match at the stream of gas. The wasps were soon just a memory, and so was the tree, which went up in flames.

The three older children also used to give each other rides in a broken-down pram. For an extra thrill, they would push it into a large patch of mud in a paddock that had been created by bulls trampling the ground. Even on the day the bulls were still in the paddock, something seemed to be protecting them, and they came to no harm.

Despite such near misses, his mum was adamant that the children should be allowed to try things and test themselves against their environment. They were particularly keen on climbing pine trees on windy days, when they had a bit of motion as well as height. As their mother saw it, a fall would be a useful lesson in how to stay on next time. Recreation often had a practical component, too. Learning to dive was great fun, but also yielded kai – food – in the form of kina. There were no goggles or masks. Willie could sometimes see the kina, but otherwise harvested by touch.

Home maintenance, plumbing and carpentry, how to light a fire, putty up a window or fix a rat hole – his mum had learnt all these things and, as the occasions arose, passed the skills on to her children. In later years, they would report frequently being surprised at what they knew, and had perhaps forgotten they ever knew, when their own children asked them how to do things. She also used to leave affirmations around the house for them. The positive ones would wish them good fortune or simply tell them to have a nice day with a feel-good message. Less cosy were the stern instructions about this or that aspect of behaviour that would be signed 'The Fuhrer'.

At Te Kaha, the children spent more time at the beach than at home. Their mother would send them off with a packet of sausages, flour and water, and a box of matches. Down at the creek they would light a fire, make takakau – Maori bread – and cook their sausages.

She would not see them again until dinnertime. One summer they even spent days constructing an elaborate Maori kainga – or village – out of beach flotsam and sand.

There was the beach and a freshwater river running straight into the sea, and Mum only saw my sisters and me when we were hungry. The adults would go fishing, and we were old enough to take care of ourselves. We camped down at the beach and stayed there, with our cousins. We had the sand village that was there for the whole holidays, and we would keep relighting the fire on it every time we went down. That made a little volcano, and it kept growing. Those were good times.

We all stayed locally. You'd go to visit a mate and someone would say, 'Oh, shall we go to the sandy beach for the day?' And we'd pack some precooked sausages from one of our houses and a bit of kai, light a fire and there was your lunch. Take a loaf of bread and stay down there all day swimming. Pakeha Mark had a little dinghy, and there used to be a bit of surf that would come in now and then, so we'd put the boat in the water and play in the waves, or at last light you'd hop in with sharpened sticks and spear the stingrays as they came into the bay to settle in the sand and rest.

Even though we had all that free time, and a pretty relaxed lifestyle, we didn't miss out on school. The first one I went to was Waima School. I liked it there. There were only two or three classes. Mr and Mrs Shaw were our teachers, and first thing in the morning she would read us a story. I did find it hard to sit still though.

We used to do a lot of different things. Come autumn, because we had lots of trees around the school, and all the leaves would drop off, there'd be no lessons in the morning. All the kids would be out raking up the leaves into big piles. And then we would play in them for the next hour or so, diving into the piles. One of our teachers had been to Indonesia and came back with an

Indonesian wife. For lunch one day they made an Indonesian meal and we had to eat it the way they do, with one hand. I'd have to do that again, years later, in Afghanistan.

I won a dog competition at Waima School when I was about six. We had show days where you took an animal, either a lamb or a dog or a calf. I took my scabby little sheepdog, Smokey. He was full of fleas and this was the first and only time he was shampooed in his whole life. He ended up smelling like apples. The old lady got some baling twine and made me a little leash for him and plaited it to make a collar. I was surprised when we won. There was a Doberman there that was a fine-looking dog, but he bit the judge. It was a buzz to come back with a ribbon and a little certificate saying I had the best dog on the show day. My eldest sister had taken her cow, which was meant to be a calf but had got too big by the time show day came around. And I think one of the other girls took a lamb.

Another time, I won a prize for my scones. Nobody helped me bake them. Mum just supervised. The things that I was good at in school were things like playing rugby and cooking. I used to love home economics, standing there and baking cakes and loaves. I enjoyed all that, because I'm not too bad in the kitchen, and I still love cooking. But that was about it for school. I persevered with everything else we did, like English and social studies and maths, but I wasn't that hot at maths, and my spelling was terrible and still is. I always say to kids: 'I suffer now because of things that I didn't learn at school and now I'm having to go back and learn them.' I am, too, because the Army gives you the opportunity to do that.

My eldest sister was always good at school and stuck up for me, even when the teachers used to pick on me. I was doing detention once, picking up gravel out of the gutter and putting it in a bucket. Then the teacher would come along and put it all back in the gutter again. It was just a menial task. My sister came along and said, 'What are you doing?'

'I'm on detention,' I said. 'I've got to do this punishment.'

27

She booted the bucket over and said, 'Grab your bag, I'm taking you home.'

We were walking away and the teacher turned up and said, 'What are you doing?'

'Are you the one making my brother do that demeaning task?' she demanded.

'He's being punished, he's on detention,' replied the teacher, but my sister walked off. I went with her and the moment we were round the corner, I gave her a big hug. 'That was choice,' I said. Thank you, sis, for looking after me.'

Later, when I was living with my father on my own, I went to the local school near where he lived called Rerekohu. I only kept up school then because you miss your mates if you don't go.

I finished school by myself as soon as I could. I didn't ask the old man. I just came home from school one day and said, 'I've finished school, Dad.'

Willie is a born hitchhiker – not only do you get to travel in different vehicles and meet new people, but there is always the potential for a small adventure. He thumbed his first lift when he was seven. It was not long before his parents split up, and the family was living on a station at Waima. Willie's parents had gone out and Willie had been left with his Aunty Tootsie. He had her daughter for company. The two had been squabbling but Willie decided he'd had enough of his cousin and said, 'Oh, bugger you, I'm walking home.'

He began trudging down the main road, and before long an old couple stopped.

'Where are you going?' asked the man.

'Oh, I'm just going up to the station,' Willie answered.

'Jump in,' the man said, and Willie did. The pair gave the little boy a piece of cake and a biscuit and he sat in their car happily munching away. They dropped him off at home and he thanked them politely and went inside.

But his parents were still away, so he made himself a meal. His mum had taught all her children how to fend for themselves even at that age. Then he went to bed. When he woke up the next morning his parents were home. And they weren't happy. His mum berated him for taking a risk by riding with strangers.

'You can't do that sort of thing,' she said, but he's been doing it ever since.

For much of Willie's childhood, after his parents separated, his father lived near the family and Willie would shuttle back and forth between his mum and dad. He might leave his mother's because something was impelling him to seek male company. He might move back because boys love their mums. But he ran away from home when his mum gave his dog to a neighbour. He set off to retrieve the pet and started hitching, dog in tow. The first car that pulled up and stopped contained his mother.

'Get in the car, son, hurry up,' she said. 'We're going home.'

'No,' said Willie. 'I'm going down to the old man's place.'

'Oh well,' said his mother, 'I'm going to have a cup of tea. I'll come back one more time and if you don't give in, then that's it.'

By the time she came back, Willie still hadn't managed to get a ride, but he had walked a lot further down the road.

'Are you getting in the car? Last chance.'

'No, see you later.'

She drove away. She was happy to give him a chance, but she was not a person to waste time on other people's stubbornness, or force them to get into a car. Willie was eventually picked up by someone he knew and managed to reach his father's place in a couple of lifts.

'What's going on?' said the old man.

'I've run away from home.'

His dad didn't mind. He was always pleased to see Willie, and his mum knew where he was. When he lived with his father, she would still come down to visit him.

With few possessions, Willie had his heart set on getting a horse from an early age. His middle sister had to do washing and ironing for a year to earn enough from her mother to buy one. And Willie, too, had to work hard to get his.

I had to cut the whole side of a hill with a slasher made out of a big meat cleaver on the end of a big long handle. Then I had to chop up all this willow into firewood. Looking back now, someone would have got paid a couple of hundred dollars or even more to scrub-cut that much and chop up the wood. I did it for 75 dollars from a local orchardist and camp ground owner, because that's all I needed to buy my horse.

I already knew how to ride, because we used to ride with my father. I was never formally taught to break horses, I just picked it up as I went along doing what I thought was right and would work. There was also a friend at Te Kaha, Dave Higgins, who used to get us to help him out by riding his horses when his girls were too young to ride them. They were mean beasts, some of them.

A fellow called Tom Baines owned two horses. I told him I wanted the stallion, and he let me have it. Once I'd got the money, my little sister and I got on her piebald, Manny, and rode all the way to Te Waiti where the horse was. It had never been broken in, and we had to chase it out onto the road and all the way back to Whanarua Bay. I chased the horse into a yard and left him overnight. The next morning when I went back, he was as quiet as a lamb.

I threw a rope around his neck and tied him to a post. Usually when something lands on a horse's head it reacts, but he didn't even pull on the rope. Then I got a big willow branch with heaps of leaves on it and started tickling him.

Tickling takes the kick out of a horse. You tickle him and tickle him until he gets used to being touched. Then you 'bag' him – hitting him with a bag. You're not hurting him, just getting him even more used to being touched. All this is before you even put a hand on him. After doing that nearly all day, I touched him myself, and he was placid. I touched his feet, lifted up his legs, and he was fine.

It was a big yard, so I put a long rope on him and started lunging him around the yard in circles with a stick, turning him one way and then the other, and he was sweet. Then I tied him to the post again and hopped on his back and he didn't buck once.

We had no bridle. The first real bridle I had was years later. Before that we plaited them out of rope, and I often ride a horse with just my jersey wrapped around its neck to control it. You can do that with most horses that have been ridden a lot. You don't need a lot of gear.

So I made a bridle out of rope, hopped on him and rode him back home. He was broken in.

And that was Blaze, the best horse I've ever owned. He would do anything for me. I could lay him on the ground. I could jump any fence or gate with him. He would pull anything. There were times when he would be in the paddock and the little kids would walk over and hang on to his legs, play under him, pull on his nuts and tail, do all sorts, and he wouldn't do anything. He never once bit me or anyone else. And he'd just stand there because he was so good-natured. There was no dirt in him; he was such a clean horse.

He even let me put a sled behind him. I pulled down part of my mum's boundary fence and used the wood to make it. I was hammering away and she called out, 'What are you doing?'

'Oh, I'm just making something, Mum.'

And she didn't take much notice. I had my ropes knotted together and got everything rigged up, and she looked out again.

'Wills, has that horse ever pulled anything before?'

'No, Mum. But I've made a sled, and I'm off to the shop.'

And that was me off down the road, galloping full tilt, taking up the whole road, because when we went round a corner, the sled would slide out into the other lane.

By the end of the ride there wasn't much wood left, so I went to get some more to make another sled, but Mum was on to it now.

'Where are you getting those posts from?' she demanded.

'From the fence.'

'What fence?'

'That fence.'

'That's my boundary fence! Find your own posts. No more wood off my fence, boy.'

So that was the end of sleds for a while. Years later, Kainui and I made sleds for our horses, and Kainui's father, Reuben, who we called the old chap and who was like a father to me, said if we put steel runners on them they would go farther and last longer. But I thought it might not be so good when you stopped, so I just used posts on mine, but Kainui used the steel.

We went down to the shop and on the way home we were galloping along when Kainui hit the brakes. The horse stopped, and Kainui and his sled slid into the horse. Well, a horse's natural reaction is to kick. And kick him it did, and took off with the sled still attached. We were picking up pieces of sled all the way home. When we got there, the horse was waiting for us at the gate. Kainui was covered in horseshoe marks from being kicked. Reuben said, 'How did it go?' and I said, 'Well, mine was all right, but I don't know about the bro's.'

Blaze was a stallion, and all stallions have the call of nature. Because he could jump any fence, I would often have to go and collect him in the morning after he had been off seeing the mares down the road. And he was an absolute dog to catch on those occasions, because he knew all these tricks.

I'd cull out all the mares and have Blaze cornered, flush up against big steel gates. You could see in his eyes he didn't want to be caught. And then, from standing, he would be straight over the gate and off, so the hound and hare chase continued.

I didn't want to cut his nuts off because I wanted a foal out of him, so I made some hobbles for his front legs out of chain with sponge around it so it didn't hurt his hocks. You would think that would stop him, but you'd be wrong.

He jumped the gate, jumped a cattle stop and hobbled all the way back to the mares. This time, they had chain marks on their backs.

So I made another set of hobbles. I figured, if it was good enough for the front legs I'd put some on the back too. Well, even that didn't stop him, so eventually he was gelded.

He was quite clumsy too, like me. Once when I was riding him, he got his feet caught up in some blackberries. He did a flip, and I flipped off him and landed on my back. Looking up, all I could see was the backside of my horse coming down, and he landed straight on top of my head. I was bouncing around making a lot of noise. My horse just got up and stood there waiting for me to stop screaming.

Matua, Kainui's brother, was riding Blaze on one of the rugged tracks up the Raukokore River when he lost his footing and went over a cliff. Blaze died instantly and the old chap had to ring up and tell me. That was hard for him. I went up there next time we went hunting, and he showed me where Blaze was. I walked down and pulled off one of his hooves. It's in my shed at home, still with the shoe attached that I had put on him.

CHAPTER TWO

HUNTER

As he grew up, Willie Apiata acquired numerous interests and skills that would feed into and fuel his abilities, both as a soldier and a man. Many of them would be accompanied by a deeply felt spiritual side, a legacy of his Maori heritage. But when he was still a teenager the spirituality gave precedence to a highly developed taste for adrenalin. After his family – a long way after his family – young Willie Apiata loved hunting and rugby.

He got his first pig when he was 14, on the day New Zealand won the Rugby World Cup. Willie was living with his father. He awoke early that morning and before the sun had fully risen saddled up one of the farm horses, Boy, got the dogs and told his father he was off.

'You're not going to stay and watch the game?' asked the old man.

'No,' said Willie, 'I'd rather go hunting.'

With just the animals for company, Willie headed to an area of native bush he thought might be productive. On the way the dogs got wind of a goat and Willie had to chase them off it. The goat was badly injured by the time Willie got to it and had to be killed.

'Go and find some pigs,' he ordered the dogs.

By the time he'd finished dealing with the goat the dogs had indeed found a pig and had it bailed up. He couldn't see them but he could hear them well enough. When he reached them, there were panicking pigs running in all directions, trying to get back into the bush.

These dogs were new to hunting too, but they had successfully bailed an old sow. Willie got down and, with some effort, managed to get the pig on its back. At 14 he was not big.

The pig, however, was big. Willie stuck and gutted it. Then he lit a fire to singe off the hair so that it could be cooked. But he was not strong enough and the pig was too heavy. He could barely roll it around on the fire and eventually conceded defeat, having managed to singe only the front.

There was no way he would be able to hoist the pig onto Boy to get it home, so he tied it to the horse's tail and dragged it onto a high bank. Then he untied the pig and led his horse around so that he stood below the pig. A bit of a heave and he was able to roll the pig onto the horse's back.

After tying everything down Willie started to head home, proud and happy. On the way, the dogs got onto the scent of another goat and caught it. Willie stopped, tethered Boy and raced after the dogs to get them away from the goat. But when he got back to where he'd left the horse, Boy had gone. Suddenly the hunter's triumph was turning into a fiasco. Tracker Willie followed the hoof marks to where Boy was waiting for him at a gate. By now, thanks to the horse's exertions, the pig was halfway off the saddle. Again, Willie took it off, tied it to the horse's tail and dragged it to another bank where he repeated his earlier manoeuvre. He reached home without further incident.

His dad was having a beer and watching the big game with his boss.

'How'd you go, son?' he asked.

'I got a big sow,' said Willie.

His father left the game and rushed out to have a look.

'What's the matter with your pig?' said his father. 'It's got hair on it!'

Not long after Willie caught his first pig, his father went out of his life for a long time, leaving him to fend for himself on the property where the old man had been working. Willie waited some days after his father had left the farm, but once he suspected his father wasn't coming back, he went to see his mother, who knew all about it, and confirmed it.

Around this time, he attached himself to another father figure, the old chap, Reuben Parkinson. Willie moved in with his family, and for the next few years would move back and forth between the Parkinsons and his mum. As with so many older men Willie has encountered, Reuben became a mentor who taught him an enormous amount; Willie became a willing apprentice, soaking up all that knowledge. Reuben was an enthusiastic hunter and consumer of pigs, an activity that came with its own rituals.

I like the smell of pigs when they're cooking. It's a really strong game smell. There's nothing better than a feed of wild pork. It's the best buzz. Everything on the pig is lovely. The first parts we'll eat are the heart, the kidneys and everything that is inside him. People say, 'All that beautiful meat – why are you eating the guts?' It's what hunters do. That's their favourite part.

When we went hunting, we never took food, because we knew as soon as we caught the pig we got to eat the stomach. The fire wasn't just lit to singe the pig – it was also lit so you could cook the heart and other parts you eat first. Being hungry really makes you hunt.

Once we just about cooked ourselves. Reuben and his boys and I were going for an early-morning hunt, but none of us had a watch. We woke up in the dark and the old chap said, 'Come on, boys, it must be nearly morning. Have a feed, grab the horses and we'll get going.'

We saddled up, got the dogs and rode into the bush. It was freezing, but we got into it. After a few hours, it was still not daylight, and it looked like it wasn't going to be any time soon.

'We must have left at about eleven o'clock,' said Reuben. 'Let's light a fire and warm up.'

We had a big kai, and the fire was so good that someone said, 'If only you could sleep on it, that would be really warm.'

So we decided to have a go. We made the fire a bit bigger, and the old chap sent us to get as much greenery as we could find. We got piles and piles of scrub and heaped it on. Smoke was coming through, but we all jumped on. I lay there thinking it was great.

Well, it was great for about 10 minutes, but then flames started coming through. We wanted to see who could stay there longest before getting burnt. We kept adding greenery, to the point where you could maybe sleep for half an hour before someone woke up screaming because they were getting cooked.

We thought it was fun, but the old chap finally had enough and told us to grab our horses, because there was still no sign of light, so we were going home.

We started picking our way back. This was steep country with only rugged little narrow tracks, but we got to the river flats when it was still dark.

The flats go along then dip down, go along and then step back up again. We decided to have a race, and, because of the layout, you would see someone ahead of you and then they would disappear when they went down in the dip. It's an unreal feeling. You're galloping along, and then the horse disappears and takes you with it. It's like going over a big bump in a car really fast, and then you scream back up the other side in absolute pitch darkness. By the time we pulled up our horses, we were all buzzing and we certainly weren't cold any more.

Before pigs, when I was small, I'd take my little foxie hunting for rabbits. They were everywhere around where we lived and he'd flush them out of the holes and we would grab them.

I hunted possums for pocket money, from when I was about 12. There was no shortage of them. Before school every morning, I'd get up, clear the traps and leave the possums in the shed till I got back from school. Then I'd dress them all up and hang them out.

I took the skins to Dalgety's in Opotiki, and left my name with them. The skins would be sent off, and a few weeks later a cheque would turn up in the mail. The first lot I sent was only seven skins, but I got a hundred dollars back. That was a lot of money.

Because they were my first ones, and I'd stretched them in any old fashion, they sent me a big folder, like a lesson plan on what to do: how to skin the possums, how to tack them out, how to get the tail off without ripping it.

I gave it a quick read and I was away. I'd already been skinning animals for a long time. I got my first knife from my father when I was about seven and had plenty of cuts on my hands to show for it. I could skin cows and sheep – it's the same process for any animal; the only difference is the size.

Where we hunted, there were also wild cows we used to go after. Kainui had a compound bow that was powerful enough to drop a full-grown cow.

38

We had to quarter them and hang them off the horse to bring them out, but the tracks were so narrow and steep it was hard on the gear and the horses. We used to bone them on the spot and leave behind only a skeleton.

We used to ride the cows too. You would set your pig dogs on them – they would hold them and the cows wouldn't move. Then we'd ride up, jump on to the cow and grab some skin and see how long we could stay on.

The other thing Reuben and his boys and I loved was rugby. The boys were my mates at school. I was into male companionship, because when you've only got girls in the family, much as you love them, you get sick of them pretty quick.

I was a small guy for rugby, but strong. Although I was little, I liked to play in the forwards because I hated sitting things out. I wanted to be right in there, where all the rough-and-tumble was going on. Kainui and I were the smallest and strongest locks on the East Coast. No one could push our scrum back.

I only ever made the 2nd XV at any of the schools I went to, but I made Tai Mitchell three years in a row. Tai Mitchell is a schools rugby competition that they have around the Bay of Plenty with teams from Rotorua, Rangitikei, Galatea and other places.

Reuben used to be our coach, and Mum was our cook when we went away and stayed on the marae to do our training camps. She also helped with fundraising, going round pubs and pestering drinkers so we could afford uniforms. She was right into it, and now my boy is playing sport I understand that, because all I want to do is go and watch him play. I suppose if I hadn't found the Army, I might have been able to become a rugby player.

The old chap – Reuben – used to train us so hard that parents would complain about it. We thought he was just preparing us properly, trying to make us fit and hard for what was to come.

'The only reason we're training hard like this is so that you fellas don't get hurt,' he would tell us.

Reuben used to drive us all on his big house truck down to a place called Maraetai to train. Three of his boys were in the team, too.

All the kids would jump out, and we would run along the beach from there to Pahaoa Marae. The sand down there is coarse and soft to run on, and we used to have to run about five kilometres – and this is boys as young as 10. Then you'd have to swim through the Kereru River, which is about 800 metres, before you got to the marae. The water was up to my chest, and there were boys in the team who were smaller than me.

Once you got there you would wait for your team-mates, then you ran to the top of the marae to do your weight training. After that you had a feed, and then it was rugby practice for the rest of the day. You had two weeks of that to build up to the tournament.

Reuben was hard, but he loved youngsters and rugby. He could recognise when they had talent, and he wanted to see them play and be good at it. We had hard times but we always had a good time. The old chap expected you to drain yourself completely every time you played. All he asked was that you give your all.

Once we beat a team, and they were too scared to play us again, because we hurt so many of their players. We had minimal injuries – bruises and a few ruck marks from sprigs – but some of them got carried off the paddock. That was because of the training Reuben had given us.

Later on, when we were old enough to be allowed a few beers, Reuben would still be with us. If we'd played a good day's rugby, he wanted to be sure we didn't miss out on having a good time afterwards. So he would be our driver, drink tea all night and make sure we got home okay.

He had mellowed out a lot by that stage. He used to be very highly strung. In any high-pressure situation he would go off like you had to see to believe. We got used to it, but to this day I haven't been yelled at by any commander or sergeant or corporal in all my years in the Army as hard as I used to get yelled at by the old chap. I've seen him swearing and yelling at people until they've started bawling and gone into the foetal position, because he was so scary.

I've seen grown men who absolutely feared him. People trembled in his presence. I've seen him walk into a pub and everyone in it scurry off like mice looking for a hole to crawl into. In his younger days he was a force to be reckoned with, and when he was older he was still a force to be reckoned with.

Despite his physical presence and hard demeanour, the old chap was a fair man who taught me a wealth of knowledge and I respected and loved him immensely.

His mum appreciated the interest Reuben had taken in Willie, especially with his own father off the scene. But she, too, knew how intimidating Reuben could be. At one point during Willie's time living with the old chap, Reuben started to talk about Willie's family in a way the boy thought was out of line. Upset, Willie went to see his mum.

'Mum, can you come over to Reuben's?' Willie asked her. 'I wondered if you could have a talk to him and remind him that you're my parent and he's not my father.'

She looked at Willie. 'I beg your pardon?' she said.

'I thought, if you talked to him . . .'

She knew she would need all her courage to have that conversation. Fortunately, courage was something she wasn't short of. So she went to see Reuben.

Reuben used to keep a legendary pot of tea – 'marae-sized' – going on the stove all day, stewing away as he added handfuls of leaves and more water to it when it got low.

'Morning, there's a cup of tea here,' he said.

She pretty soon got to the point, and told Reuben what Willie wasn't happy about.

'Wills has asked me to talk to you, because he wants to keep coming over, but he wants me to let you know that I'm his mother and I'm his parent.'

There was a pause. The only other woman known to be able to stand up to Reuben was his wife, who Willie also adored as a second mother.

Reuben finally said, 'If you've got enough guts to come over here and tell me that, then that's fine. You won't have to ask again. Don't you worry. I'll keep Willie busy with Tai Mitchell.'

Willie doesn't know for sure why Reuben took such an interest in him. There was his obvious talent for football and bushcraft, but the old chap already had sons of his own. For his part, Willie loved Reuben's stories, and was happy sitting with the pot of tea, listening to him for hours. The conversations and stories never dried up. He also missed his father a lot.

Later, when Rueben had passed on, it was as though all the pigs knew and came out of hiding, because suddenly there were pigs everywhere.

CHAPTER THREE

THRILL SEEKER

Reuben Parkinson wasn't a man to take much notice of people's complaints, and not many people will hear Willie Apiata complain about anything, except perhaps an opposing rugby team failing to front for a game. The old chap had taught him stamina and endurance, encouraged an appetite for the rush of adrenalin and activities that produced it, and helped develop the intense physicality that Willie inherited from his parents and that would stand him in such good stead when he joined first the Territorials and later the SAS.

Today, although Willie is taller than average and powerfully built, most people do not realise how big he really is. This may be because he does not use his bulk to create an impression or dominate. Until his late teens he was seen – accurately – as a scrawny boy. He didn't bulk up until he was over 17. His sisters were taller than him for longer than normal. But he didn't let it worry him too much. He knew that one day he would grow.

Until then, however, he had to put up with such indignities as being on the receiving end of a hiding from a fifth-form girl – when he was in form two. Normally he was fast enough on his feet to escape the consequences of his smart mouth, but not always. And this was one of those times. It was obvious when he got home that he had received some kind of hiding, but when asked about what had happened he merely said, 'I got into a fight at school.'

Even after he left school and was knocking around with older people, he still got picked on, and by the sort of people who wouldn't let existing injuries stand in their way. Once, when he had a leg in plaster following a motorbike accident, he was standing in a marae car park with a friend, having a cigarette. A couple of older guys who were passing looked at Willie and his mate and introduced themselves by saying, 'Hey, you tossers.'

They walked over and threw Willie's crutches in the road, where they got run over. Willie indulged in some verbal retaliation and they started dealing to him. His mate jumped in his car and drove away. Willie played possum until they got bored and left him on the side of the road. He then sought out some of his older mates.

'Look what those guys did to me,' said Willie. 'And I've got a broken leg.'

Willie's friends tracked down his attackers and administered summary and swift justice before sending them on their way.

The attackers were from the same part of the country as Willie, and he occasionally sees them around the East Coast. He's not fussed. One of his more firmly held principles is not to hold a grudge. He's good at putting the bad things behind him and moving on. And besides, the wrong had been paid for at the time.

In fact, Willie is not one to settle conflicts physically. His mother drummed into him that alcohol and violence are a particularly poisonous combination. She once even tested him by trying to provoke him to lash out, but he was too good a man for that. However, he won't stand idly by if alcohol is causing someone to embarrass themselves or their mates in front of other people. Anyone who makes that error will be quickly brought back into line.

Where he grew up, Willie got to see gang behaviour up close. Members were friends of friends, and it wasn't unusual to end up at a party with members present. He found it illuminating to see how little their actions matched their words and the staunch impression they worked so hard to create. In particular, he noted that they were as likely to turn their aggression on each other as they were on other gangs. Once at a party, a shotgun came through a window. Suddenly, apparently tough guys, who had been talking tough and hoeing into each other not long before, were cowering under the table trying to eat carpet.

'What's going on here?' thought Willie. 'Where have all these big tough men gone?' He and his mate, who were only there for the beer, had been sitting quietly nursing their drinks. Now, equally quietly, and still holding their beers, they left the party, and left the members to sort out whatever real or imagined offence lay behind the incident.

They parked at the wharf and slept in their van. When the police came by to ask what they might know about the incident, Willie managed to inject maximum humour into his version of the story, with much emphasis on the shortage of spine in those involved.

He formed an equally dismal opinion of another acquaintance

who talked him into accompanying him to Auckland with the promise of some mischievous good times. Willie had never been to Auckland before and the expedition sounded like fun. But despite much talk about what they would get up to, little interest was displayed in actually making good on the talk when they got there. Eventually, the friend scrounged enough money to pay for two bus tickets back to Opotiki.

On the other hand, men – and women – who are as good as their word, who mean what they say and say what they mean, who only say they are going to do something if they are going to do it, earn his enduring respect. People who don't try to be anybody but themselves, and who don't talk themselves up are the people who gain Willie Apiata's admiration.

Willie is also the sort of person who has sought out all kinds of thrills throughout his life.

I was well used to guns by the time I saw that one come through a window at the party. It didn't frighten me. My first gun was a .22 that I got when I was 14. I had about 30 possum skins and I traded them for a semi-automatic .22 and a couple of boxes of bullets from a dude, and that was it. I was into guns from then on.

I showed my younger sister how to shoot with that gun. We went down to the beach one day and set up a whole lot of cans, and I said, 'There you go, sis. Have a shot.' And she thought it was going to kick like a horse, but of course it doesn't, and she thought it was great. So that was it. After the first one I could hardly get it off her. From then on we would be down there shooting cans every day.

One day I went shooting up the Toatoa with my cousins who had an old .303. I'd never fired one of those before. They got an old pot and chucked it out on the stones in the riverbed and were shooting at it. One of the cousins had a shot first. He only got stones, but that was okay. The next shot hit more stones near the pot. Then he passed it to another cousin who hit the can no trouble, because it was his gun. Then he asked me if I wanted a turn. I said, sure, and lined it up and squeezed the trigger. And it kicked like nobody's business. But all you saw was the pot flying up in the air.

They thought it was a fluke, so they got me to have another shot, and I got it again. I was rapt, and I kept those shell cases for a long time. That was my first big gun. All the hunters in those days had .303s. You hardly ever saw a .308. That's probably why I hunt with a .303 now.

I try to do most of my shooting with the iron sights. A lot of people have scopes but that first gun of mine must have been a real budget item because it had the smallest scope I've ever seen. It was more like a pistol scope, and I could never use it properly. I could still shoot things with my .22, but only as long as they were close.

The weapons we get in the military are top notch and I have lost count how many different types I have fired. I get to practise with guns a lot, and I have a good eye as a result. When I'm hunting I won't shoot anything if I know I might miss or will wound the animal. We are trained to always, before we engage, identify our target properly. That is basic.

But despite all the fun I've had with guns and hunting and rugby, the best adrenalin experience I've ever had is bull riding at the Opotiki rodeo at Christmas.

You turn up at nine in the morning and pay your $15 for a ride, and then you wait. It's neat fun because you're sitting on something you have no control over at all. The only thing you have to do is stay on for eight seconds, but that eight seconds is a long time. The excitement starts in the cage when you're sitting there thinking, 'How is this thing going to react?' Some of the bulls you see at the rodeos are so savage, and I'm amazed that anyone can ride them – it takes technique as well as a lot of muscle to stay on some of those beasts.

There's no safety helmet at the rodeo. You wear your regular gears. All you've got to hold on with is one hand, and they actually strap you in there. They loop a tether around your hand and you have to hold onto it – you practically have to sit on your hand to do it.

The first bull I ever rode ran out and galloped around the ring, so it was just like riding a horse. And when the hooter went I jumped off and thought, 'Well, that was nothing much.'

On my second ride, the gate opened and the bull screamed out and came to a halt and then started doing its thing. There was no way I could hold on any longer, and I hit the dirt after about six seconds. A guy had given me his glove and said, 'This is my magic glove.' When I gave it back to him, I had to tell him it didn't work.

On my last ride, we were watching the fun, and then it was my turn. I was wearing a shirt that had 'No Fear' written on the front and 'Fear is in the eye of the beholder' on the back.

I hopped on the first bull. It was almost ready to go, when it sat down. I was about 120 kilos then. I was kicking it, but nothing happened, so they pulled me off and brought up another one and told me to get on. I had to wait for someone else to finish, and it all looked good, but just when it got to be time for us to be let out, it sat down too.

They only had one more bull, but they said they would bring him up. He was smaller than the other two, and I took one look at him and was sure I was going to squash him. But I hopped on, and they strapped me in. He was bellowing and shifting to the side. You can feel through your legs what he's feeling, and he is as tense as you. They were just about to open the gate, and he sat down too.

But this time they opened the gate anyway. The bull stood up and rocketed out of there. I've been in one drag car and a lot of V8s, but the G-force from this thing screaming out of the chute was unreal.

I was laid right back, and he came to a screaming halt before he popped me off like a cork and I was gone in mid-air. I'd been on for two seconds at the most.

I think they may have banned bull riding in some places now because of safety concerns, but I think we're losing our daredevils. And every time they have a rodeo somewhere, if I'm around, I try to get in for a ride.

CHAPTER FOUR

ROAD WARRIOR

One day, when he was 15 and legally able to, Willie told his father he was leaving school. He didn't hate school, but he didn't love it either. He did his time and got out as soon as he could, departing with little in the way of qualifications, but plenty in the way of opportunities. There are always opportunities for someone as resourceful, energetic and personable as Willie Apiata.

Like many young people his age, he had no clear idea of what he wanted to do. He enjoyed playing rugby and did so for fun; however, celebrity try-scorer was not on his list of goals. Eventually he found the Army – or rather, it found him – although he would not become a full-time soldier until becoming a badged member of the 1st New Zealand Special Air Service Group, at the age of 30, in September 2002.

Before that there would be many jobs. The Bay of Plenty horticulture industry meant there was lots of seasonal work, such as fruit picking, when he needed it, but there were also numerous spells of truck driving and the occasional period on the dole. He worked in forestry for many years, planting, pruning and thinning in some of the steep country around the coast. He liked it because it was hard, physical and challenging. The men he worked with were as competitive as he was, turning any task into a race to see who could do more or finish sooner. As for other occupations, it would be hard to find a job that's more of a contrast with an SAS member than vacuum cleaner salesman, but Willie loved his time selling vacuums around Tauranga.

When he was 18, he answered a newspaper advertisement placed by a vacuum cleaner company and was accepted for their sales training programme. On day one, the novices were put in a van and went on the road with an experienced salesman, observing how he demonstrated the cleaners to a client. Willie soon realised the best way to learn was to copy others, rather than get it out of a book. He would mimic the more experienced salespeople's techniques, then add his own unique flourishes.

However, pay was commission only – no sales meant no money. If Willie was to earn his living this way, he was going to have to sell the vacuum cleaners and sell plenty of them. That meant he had to find his own clients. He took it as a challenge and rose to it. The only way to find clients was to knock on their doors. Those who let the affable young man in soon found themselves being lectured about how much dirt they had in their home. No one ever sold a vacuum cleaner by being polite.

Willie was persuasive. This was high-pressure selling, with the demonstrations sometimes turning into a battle of wills. Would the salesman pack it in and leave without a sale? Or would the homeowner agree to buy the wretched thing just to get him out of the house? But achieving the latter was slightly complicated. Part of the sales strategy was the liberal use of little white pads to show how much dirt the vacuum would get out of the carpet. The pads would be left where they could be seen as the demonstration went on. It wasn't unusual to have 150 to 200 pads spread around a piece of carpet after a two-hour sales session. The demonstrator would insist on picking these up himself – slowly – if the homeowner was trying to get rid of him. There was also the cigarette test, in which a cigarette was put into the moving brushes of the cleaner. The brushes would remove the tobacco and leave the cigarette paper intact to show how gentle the cleaner was on your precious rug.

In later years, when vacuum cleaner sellers have called at Willie's own house, he has asked them in and let them go through their paces to see how good they are. He has noticed that sales techniques are not as high pressure these days. He sold a lot of vacuum cleaners in his time and made a heap of money for a teenager. After three months he had his own van and didn't have to do the demonstrations any more. He was running his own team of salespeople. It helped that he genuinely believed in the product. But it helped even more that this was a party-focused job as far as his colleagues were concerned. Every Wednesday to Saturday night they would be out clubbing together.

Willie also spent a period selling books. He would drive around shopping centres and industrial areas and leave books and forms for people to inspect. Then he would return a couple of days later to pick up the orders. One business he called at was a funeral director's, and the manager liked him so much he gave Willie his card and told him to call if he was ever considering another change in career direction. He was, but that was not it.

Part of the attraction of sales for Willie was that he was learning something new and practical – in fact he would apply some of these skills in his army career – and that it was so competitive. As part of the warm-up for the day, he and the other salespeople would try to persuade each other to sell a body part to them. If you could do that, even in a hypothetical exercise, you could sell anything.

The other skill Willie had that came in very useful in selling was the ability not to be deterred by knock-backs. He could handle the 99 rejections that came before the one sale.

But it was jobs that put him behind the wheel of large and powerful vehicles that found most favour with the young man.

Willie had taught himself to drive when he was 13. He and his youngest sister were sitting in the car park outside a pub, waiting for their father. Eventually the old man came out, got in the back seat and fell asleep.

'Keeps him out of trouble, eh?'

'Let's go, sis,' said Willie.

He got the keys off his father and, knowing roughly what to do from having driven tractors on the farm, started up the car. It had no clutch so he had to put it in gear and turn the key to start it.

The three shuffled along the road. Every time they got to a hill they would have to stop to put the car back in first again. When they got home, the old man wouldn't wake up, so the children left him in the car and went to bed.

'How did we get here?' asked Willie's father the next morning.

'I drove,' said Willie. And he never sat in the car park waiting for his father again.

'You going to the pub?' Willie would ask. 'How long you going to be?'

'I'll be a few hours.'

'Give me the keys, please. I'm off to my mate's place.' After a few hours, Willie would drive back to the pub and find his father.

'Are you ready yet?'

'No.'

And he would return to his mate's until his father was ready to be taken home again.

Vehicles in many varieties are an ongoing passion. The love affair has continued unabated and taken many forms over the years, from homemade Mini conversions to riding out of Hercules aeroplanes in Dumvees. But more than anything, Willie loves drag racing, with the roar of the V8s and the sight of the smoke and the smell of the fuel to stimulate the senses. A personal motoring highlight was taking part in the eighth-of-a-mile Port Road street drags in Wellington. However, an early ambition to be a racing driver was channelled into other areas, notably driving trucks. He learnt how from a rugby mate during a time when he was drifting, looking for something to do, living off the dole and staying now with one sister, now with another or with his mother.

Truck driving was hard, poorly paid work. Willie was a good driver, up to the long hours, but he hadn't been trained in how to fill in a logbook to avoid fines by underestimating the amount of time he had been driving. He scrupulously recorded all his hours, which were often well over the maximum permitted. No one had told him to do otherwise. He incurred fines for working up to 120 hours a week, surviving on two or three hours of sleep a day for days at a time.

A not unusual itinerary would be to leave Opotiki at five in the morning, drive to Tauranga, turn around and finish deliveries in Opotiki by five in the afternoon, have dinner, then pick up a new load from the Opotiki abattoir, deliver it to Tauranga, wash the truck out and get back to Opotiki again, arriving around midnight. Up again at five, and repeat the journey. Few beers were ever as well earned as the ones Willie downed after a stint like that.

He has also been involved in – or sickeningly near – more than his fair share of car and motorbike crashes.

One summer, the old chap organised for me and the guys to make some money by taking people horse riding at Waihau Bay. We were flat out every day, guiding them to the end of the beach and back.

We began hanging out with a couple we met. One night, we had been at their place having a few beers. When it was time to leave, my mate went on ahead on his bike. I had a 750 Special Yamaha I'd bought myself for Christmas, and I couldn't get it started. I kept flooding it and got left behind. My helmet was over my arm and getting in the way, so I put it on and finally managed to get the bike going.

At the same time, the old chap was driving around checking on his boys. He wanted to make sure no one had been drinking and driving. I turned a corner which happened to be where Kainui had stopped his truck. The old chap's Chevy was on the other side of the road, and he was getting stuck into his boys when they heard me screaming round the corner, barrelling down on them.

All I remember is seeing the two little rear reflectors of the truck. I dropped to the ground, crunching into the stones. The bike and I went under the truck's tailgate, and I nearly ran the old chap over but he jumped up the bank in time.

There was hardly a scratch on the bike, just a broken headlight and side cover. But one side of my body was eaten up by the road. I'd been wearing a flimsy little jacket and some track pants. I threw my kneecap out and got gravel rash all up the side. I injured my elbow, and I took two marker posts out with the side of my head and cracked an $800 helmet. I didn't know until then that they made $800 helmets. Someone had given it to me. I went to replace it and thought, 'I'm not buying one of those!'

That was where we all learnt our big lesson about not drinking and driving with motorbikes or any other vehicles. The boys came and visited me a couple of days later in the hospital, and we agreed we'd never do that again. I might have a few beers now, but never if I know that I'm going to drive. There's no way I will get myself turpsed up and jump in a vehicle.

One day I was out for a short test ride on my bike after putting a new part on it. I hit a dog and fell off, was badly gravel rashed, and had to push the bike home. I dug the gravel out and went to the neighbour's to see if he had some antiseptic. He put some stuff on that had me screaming. It was burning so much it was like you couldn't feel anything else. Then we looked at the bottle and it said to use one part to 10 parts water instead of pouring it on straight out of the bottle. So that worked and I bandaged myself up with a sheet. After a few running repairs on the bike I headed off to a party at Te Kaha.

Then the rest of the family turned up, and every one of them seemed to want to hug me. I didn't want to tell them what had happened but I had to because they wanted to know why I wasn't letting them touch me. Before I knew it they had my clothes off and couldn't believe how I looked.

I said I was fine and had done everything that I needed to, and no one could do anything else, but they dragged me to a doctor. He took my sheet bandage off, had one look and said, 'There's nothing I can do.'

And I ended up with a leg in plaster after another bike crash. I did a ramp going to a mate's place, went a little too fast and landed wrong. They were pulling out of their driveway, so they stopped and picked up my bike.

They asked me 'Are you all right?' and I told them I was fine. My cigarette hadn't even gone out. So they carried on. I didn't know my foot was broken until a week later, when I went to the doctor because I couldn't walk or put any weight on it.

My dog Dandelion used to come on the bike, and she never got hurt. I had to make her a little balaclava out of a sock to keep her head warm, though. And I stuck a piece of leather on the tank so she had something to grip.

Later, when I was working in Australia, I missed getting killed in a vehicle accident by seconds. I spent six months in 1997 working in forestry around New South Wales, planting trees and pruning. I liked it, but I missed the kai and being able to hop in my car and drive home.

One morning, we were driving to Sydney to pick up some Kiwi blokes who were coming across to work with us. The sun was just coming up, and we were on a three-lane freeway with a big concrete divider in the middle. A truck with a 40-foot articulated trailer overtook us on a corner, and as he did he almost hit us. Then, after he got around the corner and was heading down the straight, he was going so fast his trailer spun out and hit the concrete barrier. As it came back around, it only just missed our truck again and hit the other side of the barrier. The tractor unit went over.

People were starting to go to work by then, and it ploughed head on into a station wagon, which flipped over and ended up facing the other way. Everything from the windscreen forward had been wiped out. There was a woman in it, squashed against the steering wheel by the impact. She had just picked up a hitchhiker, and his face was a mess.

We got out to check on the woman. She was having trouble breathing, but we managed to get the door open and were able to pull the steering wheel off to relieve the pressure on her chest. The fire brigade turned up soon after that and an ambulance took the two away. We carried on and picked up the new guys, but on the way back they were still trying to clear the carnage. Both the woman and the hitchhiker survived.

I guess the reflexes that kick in when something like that happens are the same ones that switch on in combat or other kinds of crises. Some people act by instinct. Others go into shock and can't do a thing. I realised that when I was on the scene for another accident.

We were going to visit a friend at Kutarere. We were in my car, having a cruisey time, and as we came around a corner, a tractor fell off a bank onto the road in front of us. The driver must have been backing up and gone over the side. He fell with the crash bar across his shoulders.

We came screaming to a halt. My mate and his brother, who were in the back, sat there frozen – like they had seen death. I leapt out and ran up to see if I could help, but he had been decapitated. The wheels on the tractor were still spinning. People were starting to run down the hill, but they weren't going to be able to do anything, so I drove to the nearest house and called the emergency services.

When I was working in Wellington and living at Wainuiomata, we used to have our own little demolition derby set up, with controlled crashes for fun. There was an out-of-the-way place where hoons would go to trash their cars, and we'd go there. We used to buy *Trade & Exchange* and find $50 or $100 cars and buy them. I paid my partner $200 for her old car once so we could smash it. We would take out the windows, windscreens and any other glass, and then we had our demolition vehicles. We'd spend the whole day out there, tearing around, crashing into each other and having great fun.

We had two rules. The most important one related to safety – there was no smashing into the driver's door. The second rule was that you couldn't smash the front of the vehicle. That was so the cars would last longer. It's easy to hit the front, and if you do, you stuff the radiator, and there goes all your joy. Over in 30 seconds.

The place was surrounded by gorse. We were going around the track once and a guy was chasing me in a Toyota Corona that had a wicked set of bumpers on it. He was the only one you could hit front on, because he had these two things that stuck out and stopped his car being damaged from the front.

I was in a little Mitsubishi Mirage and he was chasing me. It had been raining and was very muddy. I had my foot to the floor trying to make a sweeping bend and get past him before he cut me off. He was going to T-bone me as I came past him on the front. I could just see his tyre coming around the corner, and I had my foot to the floor and I was yelling, 'No, no, no!' And he just missed me and ploughed into the gorse. He had one of the boys' partners with him, and all you could hear was her screaming in the bushes. Well, there was no retrieving the car from that; it stayed where it was.

My Mitsubishi only lasted two weekends. One of the boys got stuck at the bottom of this ramp we'd made on top of spare wheels, and I flew off the top onto his car. We didn't think it was dangerous, because we had our helmets on and took precautions. There was no way you could get up to outrageous speeds in the kind of vehicles we had.

My car caught fire once, too. One of the boys spun out and stalled, and as I came around the track, I stopped, stuck my car in reverse and came screaming backwards into the side of his car and wasted it. Then I went forward and did it again. When I hit him, I must have cracked the petrol tank, because it suddenly went woof and all these flames shot up!

I dived across the passenger seat – I couldn't get out my door because of the flames. And as I dived out, the whole car erupted in an inferno. Everyone was stunned. We left for the day pretty soon after that.

I would make cars, too, like the one some mates and I built out of an old Mini that I swapped for a tandem truck trailer. It had a back half made out of a Falcon and a Holden six-cylinder engine. I drove that for a long time. It was a bit like this mongrel bike I used to have too. The frame was a Suzuki PE 250 combined with an ER 250, and the seat was a whole lot of rags put into a sack and tied onto the frame. And that was all – no mudguards or muffler, or anything like that. I used to ride it everywhere until I ran it into the ground.

But my best car ever was a Holden HQ racing car. I went to an auction, took one look at it and that was it. It had bucket seats, and no back seats or lining, just steel. And it was all stickered up and lowered for the road. I must have gone through about eight diffs in that thing . . .

There are only so many cars one man can run into the ground in a lifetime. All that energy was going to take a major focus to be used constructively, and Willie would find it in the Army. For a long time, despite all his obvious talent, he would resist immersing himself fully in the Army, but he spent many enjoyable years as a 'weekend warrior' in the Territorial Force or TF.

The seed had been planted when he was at school and two soldiers visited. They had been asked by a friend, who was related to one of Willie's classmates, to call by and impress the kids. They had certainly impressed Willie when they let him ride in the truck and handle a gun. There was no epiphany, though. Willie Apiata did not suddenly realise he had discovered what he wanted to do with his life. He just thought the guys and the truck and the gun were cool. He had handled guns before, but this time was different. This time, it was made clear, the gun came loaded with responsibilities.

Years later, the seed planted that day would bear fruit when he was 16 and visiting his mates Taylor and Rangi. A Unimog truck turned up and their brother Willie T jumped off it. The vehicle was heading out to the Cape, dropping off soldiers on the way.

'Where have you fellas been?' asked Willie. 'I didn't know you were in the Army.'

'Sure we are,' said Willie T.

'How do you get on that truck?'

'Come next weekend and see. We're going again,' he said.

And that was it.

Next weekend, Taylor and Willie got on the truck for a weekend experience in the Army. Willie had borrowed a pair of pants, was wearing gumboots, and was going through one of his long hair stages. They were a raggedy bunch.

The Army gave Willie and his mates an M16, some mags, and a couple of boxes of blank rounds. They didn't know how to use any of it, but they thought it was the genuine warrior experience.

They were put in a section and buddied up with an older soldier, who they followed on patrols. On the first day, they did some stands – activities arranged around a circle, like a round robin, with a different task at each point of the compass, such as patrolling, fieldcraft, throwing grenades and laying claymores.

When practising with grenades, they had to get them into a rubbish bin. Willie missed. Taylor threw his in the wrong way and a corporal started ripping him to pieces, but he was the only one who managed to get his grenade where it was meant to go. The corporal didn't know whether to continue ripping him to shreds or say, 'Good shot, mate.'

Then they were set up on a patrol and Willie had an early experience of an Army wind-up. The group was having a small halt when they were 'attacked' by an enemy. If you had a machine gun you fired automatic, if you had a rifle you fired on semi. Willie was firing his rifle as per instructions, and having an excellent time, when his mate yelled, 'Switch to automatic, switch to automatic!' Willie switched and started mowing the enemy down (in his imagination, at least) when a section commander came screaming over and started bellowing at him for firing on auto. It was a salutary lesson on whose instructions to follow when you are in the Army.

At the end of the weekend, everyone collected their gear, tidied themselves up and had a few beers before being taken home. Back then, three or four Unimogs would go to Whakatane to pick up the troops and take them to training. These days, there are far fewer young men spending weekends with the Territorials. Willie did two buddy weekends with his mates, but he was 16 and too young to join officially. As soon as he turned 17 he would sign up.

He bonded with Bravo Company even before basic training, on his first annual camp. This had it all: bush, weapons, explosives, armoured vehicles and challenges every step of the way. He loved it.

They railed up armoured personnel carriers and Scorpion tanks to the Mamaku Ranges, and I went out to be the enemy for the skill at arms competition. We spent the first half of the day sitting on a mound where soldiers could see us. Then there would be a 'hasty ambush', where you see the enemy advancing, ambush them, lay everyone out and hose them down. They get assessed and given points.

At lunchtime we swapped, and we became the enemy for the section attack. Our defensive position was behind a log. They would send a party out to recce where they would put their fire support, which way they would advance and how they were going to assault. There were lasers on the rifle barrels and your vest beeped if someone hit you with it. Then you had to lay down and die.

With most of them, you would hear the branches snapping every step of the way as they came up on the right or left flank. Bravo Company were the only ones who came straight at us. I've never seen so many smoke grenades and thunder flashes thrown. We were under the log taking cover, and before we could stick our heads out they had annihilated us. It was the best assault I've ever seen.

After that, we did a big 'advance to contact' using APCs. The idea was that we would have small contacts – encounters – with the enemy. But it rained. It started raining on day one as soon as we stepped off the start line, and it rained for day after day. The ambush pit was full of water and we were sitting there in rain that bucketed down all night until the next day, waiting for the enemy to walk past. I think they passed us twice but we couldn't see them or hear them, because it was so dark and the rain was so heavy. You can't shoot what you can't see, so we never contacted anyone that night.

What made it worse was that another guy and I were hot bagging – taking turns in the same sleeping bag. When you hot bag, you take off all your wet gear, because the only way you can keep warm is to keep the bag as dry as possible. That's about the only luxury you have in the field. So I would take off my boots and it would be nice and dry, and I'd sleep a bit and then get woken up to have my turn back on duty. But the other guy climbed in the bag after me with his muddy boots and wet gear on. So when I came back and took off all my gear and got in the bag, all I felt was mud. Mongrel. But you keep that stuff to yourself.

One of the boys got hypothermia. He lost the plot and was walking around in his underwear and tee shirt in the rain. They threw him into my sleeping bag and he got taken out. But he got taken out with my sleeping bag. So then I didn't even have a wet bag.

For part of the exercise, we did a big attack on an enemy position. That was the first time I had seen Scorpion tanks. I was a runner for the platoon and the nearest one to the tanks. It was nothing but mud and puddles. I was standing right next to a tank when it fired its big gun. All I remember is getting out of a huge puddle with my ears ringing. It was awesome.

Eventually, we got to a mud hill where everyone stopped. I think it was our second week of rain. My job was platoon runner – going around all the sections, taking them anything they needed, and making sure everyone was okay. I didn't have a moment to do anything for myself or set up where I was going to stay.

Some of the boys dried out their clothes on the APC mufflers. They would put their sleeping bags on the pipe and the bags would blow up like balloons and get warm and dry. The platoon sergeant and I made ourselves a two-man hootchie, layering it with ponga fronds to keep the wet out. And then my replacement sleeping bag turned up.

Comparison is often made between the forces and the sort of gangs Willie knew from around the East Coast. When Willie was awarded his VC, newspaper cartoonist Jim Hubbard made the link explicit with a drawing showing a Black Power gang prospect being told that it was Willie who had 'insignia worth looking up to'.

I laughed when I saw that cartoon, because it was the Black Power who dropped me off when I went to join the Territorials.

I had been given a date to be at the Army Hall in Whakatane. I was dressed to the nines. I was wearing my best jeans, because I thought it could be the last time I got to wear them, and had the holey ones I used for shoeing horses on over the top, and my favourite denim jacket. My hair was still down past my shoulders.

I hit the road early in the morning and hitched to Opotiki. Then I got another ride a bit further along to Waiotahi Beach. I had just lit a cigarette, when I heard a Ford Goldflash roaring down the road. It was full of four massive Black Power members, and it came to a screaming halt right next to me. One got out of the front seat, walked around to the back and ripped the door open. He had to wrench it because the car was so beaten up. Another one got out and said, 'Wanna ride?' I said, 'Oh yeah,' and jumped in.

I was a little guy squeezed in the back of the car between two big patched members with another two in front. They had a joint going and offered me some, but I said, 'No, no, not for me thanks, I'm going to join the Army today.'

'Choice, bro, we'll drop you off at the hall,' said the driver.

ABOVE: At home in Awakoko – mucking around in the 'Blue Angel'.

BELOW: Exercising Dave Higgins' horse. This little pony was pure evil and threw me off about two seconds after mounting him.

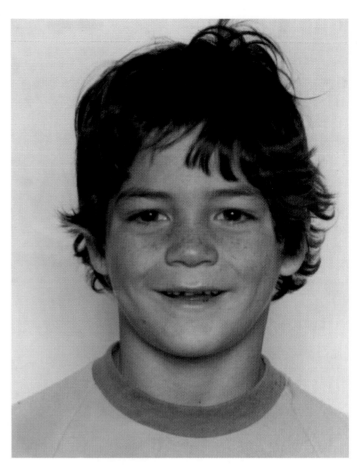

ABOVE: Waima School, Taheke – 7 years old.

BELOW: The entire Waima School (Kaikohe) in 1980.

ABOVE: Awakoko (Te Kaha) – 12 years old.

BELOW: Grandpa Jim harvesting the kumara at Awakoko.

APANUI TAI MITCHELL REPS 1984

Back Row: PHILLIP KINGI, PATU KEREI, MAHAKI WAITITI, CHIBO DELAMERE, CEFI McDONALD, CRAIG PETERS, PITA MAANGI, PATARANA KOOPU, ROWEN CALLAGHAN.
Middle Row: WAIKURA HEYBLOEM, RUEBEN PARKINSON, KEVIN FIELD, TAWHAI WAITITI, WILLIAM EDWARDS, WILLIAM APIATA.
Front Row: LANCE KARIKARI, HURAE CLIMO, TAYLOR TANGIRA, HEMI MOREHU (Captain), CLINT SMITH, MARK WILLIAMSON, GEORGE HOUKAMAU.
Managers: KEVIN WHEATON, MIKE LOADER.

ABOVE: First year in the Tai Mitchell competition representing Te Kaha and trotting out as blindside flanker.

BELOW: Horsing around with my sisters.

ABOVE: School holidays – the other kids and I created a volcano village.

BELOW: Camp 'Running Smooth'.

ABOVE: Dandelion geared up in a balaclava I made from a sock.

BELOW: 17 years old and just completed my first Territorial Force Annual Camp as a recruit in training.

INSET: My horse Blaize and the sled I made out of mum's boundary fence.

ABOVE: Christmas Holidays 2007 – Hunting with my son who took this photo.

INSET: The 'mini'.

BELOW: Overseeing progress for the feast on New Year's Eve, 2007.

ABOVE: Diving at Pari Pari – Whanarua Bay.

BELOW: Crayfishing off Wellington on the *Sandra J.*

And they took me right to the door. At the Whakatane Army Hall we pulled up outside the hangar door. It was open with the Officer Commanding and cadre standing inside it.

My Black Power driver whipped the car around sending a cloud of dust and stones flying everywhere, and the guy in the front seat got out and ripped open the door for me. I shimmied out.

'Cheers, bro, thanks very much.'

'Good luck, boy, catch ya later.'

And off they went.

'Who the hell are you?'

'My name's Willie Apiata.'

'Yeah, we heard about you coming in here today.'

'That was my last ride getting to Whakatane,' I explained.

And they took me inside, where I signed my life away. You can either put your hand on the Bible or make an affirmation, and because I'm not religious I made an affirmation.

I found out the Officer Commanding was from Opotiki.

'What time are you heading back, sir?' I asked. 'Any chance I could catch a ride?'

'How did you get here?' he demanded.

'I hitched.'

'Well, you can do the same to get back.'

I wasn't impressed. I'd just signed my life away and he wouldn't even give me a ride home.

'See ya then,' I said.

'Just before you leave,' he said, 'the person you need to be when you show back up in this army, boy, has to have cut that hair and got rid of those clothes.'

I walked out of there and hitched back home and told my mum what I'd done.

CHAPTER FIVE

SOLDIER

When Willie joined the Territorials, the minimum annual commitment a part-time soldier had to make was 21 days a year. A couple of years, he failed to make even that number due to work commitments. Although the three weeks entitled a TF member to a gratuity, Willie was occasionally committed to making money elsewhere. If he stayed away too long, on the other hand, he started to pine for the Army and the satisfaction he found there. He would always come back.

Had he joined the regular Army when he was a teenager he would now, in his mid-30s, be nearing completion of 20 years' service. But he didn't, because he liked civilian life too much back then, and he enjoyed the freedom of being able to move back and forth between the two realms. But he was beginning to find himself. That process would not be complete until he was finally badged as an SAS member, but when he joined the Territorials he knew, almost by instinct, that he was on the right track.

The first training was a seven-week course – three weeks basic and four weeks Corps – in Waiouru. The first part of it was drill and barrack inspection. He hated – and still hates – drill. None of the training was easy, and no one went easy on the new recruits. These days, soldiers can complain if they feel like they're getting a hard time, but not back in the 1980s. And that's how Willie ended up confined to barracks – CB – for insubordination.

We were out in the field and sleeping in two-man tents. It had been a great day, we had learned heaps and it was time to get our kit out for the night. Then it started snowing. That was the first time I'd seen snow. My mate and I were in our long johns, and we didn't want to have to go outside for a cigarette, so we had a smoke in our tent.

What we didn't know was that our instructor was walking around the tents, checking that everyone was all right. He opened the flap of our tent and all he could smell was the smoke wafting out.

'You guys have been smoking in your tent. Get out here,' he ordered.

We stood there at attention for about 40 minutes – freezing in our socks and long johns – while he went around and checked the rest of them. Then he came back to us and said, 'I'll deal with you guys in the morning.'

The next day, we were to start at eight o'clock, but the instructor came around at half past five and was throwing thunder flashes and smoke generators, and firing guns. We woke up to smoke grenades rolling into our tent. My mate got up and was off with the tent wrapped around him. I was left behind half in my sleeping bag. And we were both choking our lungs out from the smoke.

You couldn't see a thing. I got my shirt, trousers and boots on, and I managed to get hold of my webbing and my rifle, but I didn't have my laces done up, and my sleeping bag and tent weren't packed like they were supposed to be. You're meant to be able to pack up all your stuff ready to go quickly, but we didn't have enough time.

Some of the things we had to do and get right, as part of our normal routine, were out of control. For instance, we had to make bedrolls into 'hamburgers'. You have the mattress and the blankets, and you arrange it so you have a grey blanket, a sheet, a grey blanket, a sheet, a grey blanket. Then you have another one wrapped around the outside, so it looks like a burger. And it's got to be exactly straight. If you didn't get that right, it would be thrown across the room and you would have to start all over again. Your mates wouldn't be too happy if they thought they'd be wearing some of the trouble you'd got into because you couldn't do something properly.

We got marched around and back again, and when we got back they inspected what we had left behind. All the other tents had some little thing wrong, like a broken peg, but we had ration packs, thermo mats, sleeping bags, clothes – you name it, it was spread all over the place. It wasn't a good start. And we hadn't even been charged yet.

'Whose is this bed space?' growled the corporal. 'Get out here, you two mongrels! What have we got here? An absolute disaster.'

When we got charged, there was a Major who I would swear was seven feet tall. He was sitting down, and he was at eye level with me. And his offsider was a little guy who looked like a hit man. But you would swear he had as much fire in him as the big guy. The Major talked to my mate first.

'Why did you join the Army?'

'Discipline, sir.'

Then he looked at me.

'What about you?'

'Discipline.'

'I'll give you mongrels discipline!' he roared at us, leaning over the table. 'Seven days CB – confined to barracks. See how you like that!'

Then we got marched away by the offsider, and he tore us to pieces again outside. It was the same routine, except this time the guy telling me off only came up to my chest.

The corporals supervising you take turns because one dude wouldn't be able to stand doing the whole thing. They use up every spare moment you have. You get up at five and start whatever punishment you've got. It might be having so many minutes to get back to your barracks and get dressed in whatever he tells you to get dressed in. It could be long johns and shorts, or a Batman suit with a blanket tied around your neck, or you could have to put on your best dress – your number ones, boots and all.

And the areas where you met the guy varied, because they use the whole camp for punishment. A lot of it is done when it's dark. There's the mad mile, where you have to run from your barracks all the way to one of the ranges. You can barely make the time they give you, and there's always something extra you have to do to get it right. I had to do the mad mile with a cup full of boiling water. By the time I got there, the cup was empty, so I reached down into a drain and filled it up.

On one of the days, there was a barbecue and a few beers for the end of basic, but because I was on punishment I wasn't allowed to enjoy it. You're not supposed to have any fun. You're a bad bugger until you've finished your time. I had to stand outside looking through the window and watching my mates having a feed and a drink.

By the time I got back to my room after having my own dinner, all the guys who had been celebrating had done something wrong, and now they were getting punished just like me. They were having a room inspection out on parade. That's when you empty the whole barracks and set things up out on the parade ground exactly how they are in your room. The whole design of your barracks is laid out: beds, wardrobes, tallboys, lowboys – you name it.

When I got back, all I could see was furniture being taxied out to the parade ground. I looked in my room and all my gear had been taken out too.

They broke many a man doing CB. Some injured themselves and got a medical chit or a light duties chit, which meant they went into the office and polished trophies. We spent one night on parade shifting a whole metal pit. You would fill up your pack with as much gravel as you could carry, and then you had to run down to another area, about two or three hundred metres away, empty it out and run back. You did this all night, over and over again. And once you'd put enough gravel over there, you had to bring it all back. There was no point to it. It was purely to punish you.

After a few days, everyone else had finished their punishment or been injured, and I was the only one left on CB. I was a lonely old soldier running around the camp. I even did an obstacle course, when it was snowing, going through all the obstacles by torchlight. I went down into the muddy drain, which was up to my neck. You slide down into the mud, and you can't get out, because there's barbed wire on the top. The drain gets smaller and smaller as you go along until you have to leopard crawl to get out to one of the bridges and duck down into it to get under the bridge. Then you have to throw a grenade, get out of there and double down to the nearest fire hose, standing there freezing while the guys hose the mud off you.

Then the corporal told me I had 15 minutes to meet him at the range fully dressed in my PT kit, and I was off again. You could be doing it until one in the morning, every night and every morning for those seven days, right up till breakfast time because you've still got to do your normal duties. Punishment is on top of that. When you finish for the night, you might still be up till three, ironing your gear because it has to be perfect for the morning.

On the seventh day, most of the guys went to church, a lot of them for a bit of a nap and the cake and bikkies. But on my seventh day, they had closed the grenade range and were setting up a new one, and I got to spend Sunday filling sandbags for the new range.

There's nothing like that in the Army now. They've had to move and change. That was the worst seven days of my life, and I almost hit the wall. As a young fella, I was asking myself, 'Is this what it's all about?' I kept thinking, 'I've got so many days to go. I've just got to grin and bear it.'

And in a way I was used to it. It's how I was brought up on the farm. The next four weeks of training – the Corps training – was what I was looking forward to because on the Monday we were going into the field, where you practise everything: formations, patrolling and assaults.

When we were first in the field they had us all lined up. It was freezing because it was still the middle of winter, but the snow was all right as long as you didn't touch it. Once you did, you were wet and it was impossible to get dry.

'All those who haven't seen snow, put your hand up,' said one of the trainers. 'Be honest. Get over here. Right, you buggers, make yourself a good old snowball. And all you guys who have seen snow, stand still at attention. Right, start smashing those snowballs at them!'

When we did ambushes in training, we had to lie for hours in the freezing cold, waiting for someone to come past. By the time we could get up, we were as stiff as a folded piece of cardboard. I enjoyed the navigation training, though. You have a walker with you, who's a supervisor who knows where you are supposed to go. We were looking for an ammo tin that had the grid with co-ordinates for the next checkpoint we had to find.

But the walker put us wrong. We were heading towards the first check-point and he told us we'd gone past it and turned us around. We could see from our maps we hadn't gone far enough. But he told us we were wrong, so we went and searched where he said and couldn't find it. We were up on the high country looking down, and could practically see the three-dimensional image on our map. We knew where we needed to go, so we pushed further along to where we thought it was, and then we found it.

No one thanked our walker that day. But we were young and fit. All we had to do was put a bit of pace on and away we went. At the next checkpoint, we left the walker behind.

Near the end, we had to do a stretcher carry all the way to the next stand. There was a Pacific Island guy in the group who was so placid we had been trying everything we could to get him to show some aggression. He got chosen to be on the stretcher, and he was the biggest guy in the group. That's when he changed. 'It's all right, boys. I might enjoy this,' he said. And then he started to abuse us, swearing and insulting us at every step. We didn't even know he could swear until then. But he kept it up all the way to the end. At the time a lot of what we had to do did not make a lot of sense to me. When it was all finished and I had a chance to think about it I realised that everything we had done had a reason and I learnt a lot from the experiences I had. That is the Army way, they make the fundamentals stick so that they become second nature when you are in high-pressure or difficult situations.

Right from these very first days in the Army, Willie began to be noticed by his superiors. At this time, he came to the attention of a charismatic man who would remain important in his life, a staff sergeant Willie describes as 'the nastiest punisher that I've ever met and a legend'. Like most of those who have earned Willie's respect, this staff sergeant, George, a former SAS member, was an older man from whom he could acquire a great deal of valuable knowledge. Willie was not someone who tried or wanted to draw attention to himself, but in this group he stood out for his size, his enormous interest in and eagerness to learn about everything that was going on, and his willingness to have a go at anything. And he had plenty to learn, as far as George could tell.

He had to learn to keep his boots clean and tuck his trousers in. He had to learn how to hold his weapon, and where to look in relation to the weapon; that his eyes should be facing the same way as his weapon, so that if he saw something he needed to shoot, he wouldn't waste time lining it up. He had to learn how to react to fire and the reasons why; how to react if there was something out there where he couldn't see it – slowly, by watching it. He had to learn that if someone was going to shoot at him from behind a tree he didn't have time to aim one good shot; he should riddle the tree with enough fire to cut it down. And he had a terrible time getting his footwork right on the turns in the weapons cadre. If you are a man with a gun and you need to turn to engage someone, you have to be sure you have a firm foundation, or you are likely to miss or fall over. Willie always seemed to perform an odd waltz on his turns and get himself into a knot, but he and George persisted and succeeded in the end.

He learnt all these lessons well.

And those around him also learnt about an appetite for food that is little short of a miracle of nature. It was at this time that George gave Willie the nickname 'Mudguts', still in common use. On one occasion his appetite intersected with his duties when he was deployed as a recon member in a group sent to observe a cookhouse. Next morning, before first light, the group reported to George, who wondered why they all suddenly appeared to have put on weight and were bulging out of their clothes.

'What the hell have you fellas been doing – eating or something?'

'No, no, no, Staff. We got some food.'

'Well, take it all out, put it here.'

The not very abashed recruits pulled out bread, eggs and bacon. They were reminded that it belonged to the company, not to them; and that their job was to observe, not steal.

That incident also displayed a mild cunning streak in Willie, which is not out of place when safely harnessed within the disciplines of the Special Air Service. Especially when, as his superiors also noticed, it is accompanied by another bedrock tenet of SAS culture: the highest personal integrity.

Anything mischievous Willie undertook was usually a prank. If something went wrong and he was responsible, he would always front up quickly and say, 'I did it' and probably add, 'I also did this. Did I do wrong? Was this good?' Sometimes, what he had done was very good. Other times, such as when he helped himself to others' rations, it was less good. But he only needed to be told once.

On top of that, he was tremendously fit. If he was asked to dig a hole, he would keep digging until someone told him to stop, and he would laugh and smile while he was doing it. But he also helped and encouraged the weaker trainees, or those who were starting to tire. And that appetite of his helped power an unusually high level of personal strength.

On their Longest Day Exercise in Whangaparaoa, which involves competition between sections, Willie had been paired with a female soldier who came to just above his waist. They were moving through some manuka which was about the same height. As they started to fall behind, partly because she couldn't see where they were going, Willie picked his partner up and carried her to the next stand. It was no different from what happens on pack marches where, if a man is lagging behind, one of his mates will carry his pack as well as his own to help the whole team get there. You have to be immensely strong to perform either generous act.

Staff sergeants involved in TF training see hundreds of promising young men, some of them as capable as Willie. But many of those individuals never realise that potential. At this stage, Willie was nothing but potential, and there was no guarantee it would ever be fulfilled. The spark was yet to catch alight, and he was a long way from becoming the man who would perform the remarkable feats that lay ahead of him. But he was off to a good start.

At the end of training the new recruits took part in a march out. Willie invited his mum to come down to see it. She did and immediately got lost. Waiouru consists of large areas of concrete and numerous buildings and parade grounds that all look the same. Willie found her driving around in circles. It was the smallest of glitches. Willie took his mum out on the eve of march out. It was a memorable night. For one thing, he hadn't had a drink for nearly two months. For those weeks, the trainees had kept a 'dob book'. Anyone who stuffed up at any point was fined. By the time of the march out there was $700 asking to be put across a bar. They went to town and proceeded to spend it.

However, there was a curfew to keep everyone in good shape for the next day. The platoon sergeant instructed the group to finish their drinks and get ready to march back to camp at 10.30. They weren't at their most disciplined by then, and the attempt to bring some order to the exercise by getting everyone to whistle ended in raucous disharmony.

Drinking was part of the culture then and now, but the Army tried to teach its members how to take a responsible approach to drinking and still have a good time. When Willie joined he was taught the maxim 'work hard, play hard and gears before beers'. Soldiers might spend weeks out in the field and be exhausted and worn down by the time they get back. However, they still have to get all their gear cleaned, dried and packed away before they can even think about cracking open a beer.

Willie had done well so far. He had distinguished himself in his seven weeks of training, and he had borne a particularly tough week of discipline without whining. His willingness to be platoon runner at the expense of his own comfort – and sleeping bag – was typical of his attitude. Throughout his career it has been observed that he is happiest when he has something to do. If there is nothing for him to do, he will go out and find something. If there is something for him to do, he will do that plus a little bit more.

One TF training exercise was a major company attack on an enemy position. The weather had finally cleared, and everyone would be able to see what they were doing. Willie waited patiently with Bravo Company for their commander to turn up and put them in position so they could start advancing. George was there acting as an 'umpire' for the day, determining the likes of whether or not people had been annihilated by the machine guns firing their blanks or had survived and could stay on the attack.

It didn't take long for things to turn chaotic. Another Willie – Willie T – came under fire. He looked up and saw George telling him he was officially out of the exercise. Willie didn't know how to use a machine gun but he found one and some cover and opened fire. At one point the gun stopped working. 'Dead' Willie T came alive and started barking instructions as Willie frantically tried to get the gun to shoot.

Then an APC burst onto the scene, ploughing through the barbed wire. Willie tried to get through, too, but only managed to get himself tangled in it. The APC then backed up to reorient itself for attack on another enemy position. As it did so, it took Willie with it. Eventually, someone with a heart of gold threw the young man some wire cutters and he was able to free himself. By the time he caught up with his comrades, they had won the day. The battle was over.

After the exercise, all the battalions stayed on in Tauranga doing charter parades in nearby towns, culminating in a military tattoo in Tauranga itself. A thousand soldiers plus pipers marched through the city to perform. For Willie it was the perfect climax to the thrilling experience of a big military exercise.

He knew it was going to be something special and rang his mum to persuade her to come and see the show. She had, after all, been a devoted supporter of his military career from its earliest days. On occasions when men were allowed to invite someone to a function and Willie was asked who he would be bringing along, the answer was invariably 'my mother'. She threw herself with gusto into everything from the polite chitchat through to the target shooting. No one queried Willie's choice. To meet his mum was to love her.

However, what was different about this particular visit was that she was going to be playing a crucial part in a clandestine military operation – spiriting Willie and some mates out of camp for a night on the town. They were in their tent, getting dressed to thrill, when she turned up in her little red Starlet. She was invited in for a final briefing on arrangements for the night ahead when someone looked out and saw the Regimental Police approaching. His mum, who is not a big woman, was stashed into a sleeping bag and had the cover pulled over her head just in time.

A Regimental Police head appeared through the tent flap.

'It stinks of perfume in here. Do you guys think you're going somewhere?'

'No, no, no,' everyone swore and he left.

She emerged from the bag. 'Well, son, the perfume's certainly not coming from me, so it must be you boys,' she said.

Willie told his mother where to have her car in about 20 minutes' time for them to rendezvous with her and head to town. At the appointed time, everyone was in their agreed positions. Willie got to the car first and jumped in, yelling, 'Start the car, Mum.' They then drove to where the others were hiding behind some rubbish bins.

Looking back, no one can quite understand how everyone managed to fit into the little old car. His mum, who was driving, was squashed against the door, and Willie sat in the middle, changing gears for her. Nevertheless, the team reached their target and achieved their objective. The others wanted to stay on but Willie decided to head home early. His mum dropped him off at the far end of camp and he leopard crawled all the way back. He ended up soaked, but if there was one thing he knew about life in the Territorials by now, it was that you spent a lot of time getting wet.

Although he and the others made it safely back that particular night, there were other times when short-term escapees were not quite so discreet in returning to where they ought to be and paid the price. Going AWOL, even briefly, isn't always a lot of fun, especially if you get caught by someone with a reputation as the 'nastiest punisher' ever.

One night, after some weekend training, there had been beers in the garrison. Willie went to bed, but some of the others wanted to carry on in town. They had been warned by George that there was no leave and if they ignored the rule and were caught they should be prepared to suffer. Around 4 a.m. Willie had been up for legitimate reasons and noticed on his way back to bed that the staff sergeant's light was on. He also knew that some of his comrades who had gone to town were still not where they were supposed to be. They had to get past George's window when they got back. He was drinking tea and patiently waiting for them.

The first of the absconders to return went to the toilets, where he got undressed before walking past George's window in his underwear, to all appearances having spent the night where he should have. The others, however, perhaps with their judgement somewhat clouded, ambled past looking for all the world as though they had been out for a night on the town.

'Kia ora, you buggers,' called George. 'I hope you've all had a good night. It's not over yet. Get inside, get changed and come back here.'

Their weekend of hell began there and then. The group spent the rest of the night and all weekend taking sandbags down to the nearby water's edge, filling them up and ferrying them back to the Army Hall.

CHAPTER SIX

FISHERMAN

Of all the civilian employment Willie has had, the work that suited him best was fishing. It combined the outdoors, hard physical labour and, perhaps most importantly for the man known as Mudguts, the acquisition of large amounts of food. It also afforded similar rewards to those he got from hunting – the thrill of the chase, and the catch. And he even got paid to do it.

Willie had been with his partner, whom he met when they were at Te Kaha School together, since his 21st birthday. He had followed her to Wellington when she moved there for work. She had a job, but he was on the dole and looking for work himself, reading the Situations Vacant columns religiously, and turning up at the Social Welfare Department regularly to scan the boards for a job that might suit his skills.

He rang one advertiser, Dave Woods, who was looking for someone to help him out crayfishing. Willie loved crayfish. Woods already had some other applicants to see, and when he told Willie he would call him back, Willie's heart sank. He knew what 'I'll call you back' meant only too well from his days trying to shift vacuum cleaners. He was right, too, although at least Woods did pick up the phone to give him the bad news.

'I'm sorry,' said Woods. 'I've chosen another guy because he's a little bit older. My last one was a young guy and he wasn't punctual enough. He kept turning up to work drunk.'

Willie could be as punctual and sober as anyone when he wanted to be, but for now he could do little more than thank Woods politely for bothering to call. But it turned out age is no barrier to intoxication. When the lucky older applicant turned up to work drunk, Woods gave him his marching orders and Willie moved in to fill his place on the two-man crew.

Although Willie's crayfishing experience was little to zero, Woods didn't have to teach him a lot. He compensated for his lack of experience with strength and energy, and he had relevant skills in other areas. Making bridles and other work with horses meant he was a dab hand with ropes. He already knew how to splice them, and he had a repertoire of knots. He soon learnt how to build the crayfish pots.

On such a small crew, men have to be compatible and able to work closely together like a well-oiled machine. There's no one else to turn to or buddy up with if you're not getting on while out at sea and hours from home. Willie may have had down days, but his boss only ever saw a cheerful workmate. Many people who know Willie well say they can't imagine him being in a bad mood.

If 90 per cent of success is turning up – especially sober – Willie was a hit from the start. The work was erratic, depending on the weather in particular. A lot of it was done on call, but he was always ready when the call came. He has a good ability to read people and work out what is important to them. In this case, obviously, punctuality was a priority. He made sure that if he was ever going to be late to meet Woods, he would call and let him know first.

It was tough, demanding work – Willie's favourite kind. The waters around Wellington meant the voyages were anything but cruisey. Woods would be at the wheel and Willie would stack and clear the pots, bait them and lob them back over the side. The crays themselves were a handful, some weighing in at around five kilos, about the size of a small dog. Willie used to warn friends or family who were coming to visit that he would serve them up a crayfish they wouldn't be able to eat in a sitting. And he was right.

Willie would make his own lunch every day, to be sure he had enough fuel to get him through a shift. That meant about eight sandwiches and some cake which he was always happy to share. He claims Woods put on weight while working with him. Groper heads were used for bait, but Willie would sometimes take a few of the leftover ones home to boil up for himself, consuming eyes and all.

Fishing boats, it can reasonably be said, are neither the tidiest nor the cleanest of places. They are more like a bloke's shed on the water. But Willie, who is naturally both clean and tidy, and who tried to go that extra yard on the boat just as much as he did on his TF training exercises, obviously didn't know this.

Woods first realised he had someone out of the ordinary for his crew on the day he went to town on an errand, leaving Willie alone on the boat. When he came back, the vessel had been tidied up and all the smocks and aprons were folded in smooth squares and stacked in neat piles. And the dishes were done.

'What next?' wondered Woods.

It wasn't long before Willie's stamina manifested itself. Normally, work such as pulling in the pots is done on the side of a boat that the wind is likely to be coming from. A constant barrage of spray hits that side, as though a high-pressure fire hose is permanently trained upon it. Most workers stand side-on to the spray and cover up as much as possible with hoods or caps, leaving only a small gap to see through. Willie, however, would work with his face thrust directly into the foam, like a dog with its head out a car window. By the time work was finished, his moustache would be white with salt crystals. 'It keeps me awake,' was his explanation. Another explanation is that in any environment, at any time, Willie Apiata will try to find a challenge for himself and exceed his own expectations, which are usually higher than anybody else's.

Bad weather was equally unconcerning. The return trip on the harbour was always one of the roughest stretches on any day, and one of Willie's jobs was to clean the boat at the end of a trip. He always did it meticulously, and in order to save time would try to have the cleaning finished before he and Woods got back to the wharf. If that meant he had to be outside cleaning in pitching waves and howling wind, then that was what he would do. Woods often worried he would lose his zealous crewman, but could only get him inside to safety by issuing a direct order.

Crayfishing hours varied but usually involved early starts and mid-afternoon finishes. Most people, like Dave Woods, would then have at least a nap before heading into their evening, but Willie, who had the return trip between home in Wainuiomata and town to do every day, was more likely to have a feed and take his dogs for a run to the water tower. Or take a $50 car out for some fun with his mates. They benefited from the perks of his job too.

The boss said, 'You're allowed to take six crayfish off the boat every day.' So I would take them home for a feed for my neighbours. I called my neighbourhood my five nations. We had Indians, Iranians, Samoans, an old Pakeha couple across the road, and right next door to me was a skinhead – all his hair shaved off and a Freddie Krueger tattoo on his scalp. Plus the noisy cars. My partner would come home from work, and I'd be there hanging out with these guys. I used to give them all crayfish and fish, and they were really good neighbours. We had veggies from the Indonesian guy. The Iranians used to give me bottles of wine. The other guy used to do wood turning, making bowls on a lathe. I'd be over at their place giving them some fish, and I'd say, 'Can you make us a bowl, mate?'

I liked living there, because I wasn't in town. You couldn't see the city; you had to drive over the hill to do that. We had the beach and the coast.

Willie stayed with Woods for two years, only leaving when Woods decided to get out of crays and into charter fishing. Willie worked at a fish yard for a while before Dave Woods put another friend with a vacancy on to this top-notch worker.

Don McLeod's name takes its place alongside those of Reuben Parkinson, TF staff sergeant George, and a few others in that list of older men who Willie admired and learnt from. McLeod was 10 years Willie's senior, the tough, rough and hard-living picture of a man's man. It didn't hurt that he was also an enthusiastic hunter. He did long-line fishing, which is even more demanding than heaving cray pots about.

Long lines are fed out mechanically – if anything goes wrong they can take the fishermen with them, which is why there must always be at least two people on a boat. The lines have hooks spaced at regular intervals. When they are pulled in they are, if you are having a good day, weighed down with fish that have to be removed from the lines which are then cast again. When things are going well, it's hard and fast work.

Every night McLeod would listen to the weather forecast and decide if he and Willie would go out the next day. If they were, Willie would drive into town in the morning, meet Don, pick up the bait and they would drive to the boat. Depending on the tide, work could start anywhere between 5 and 7 a.m. McLeod took care of things up front, and Willie looked to the ropes and lines.

But the new boss and his young assistant had more in common than an interest in fish and hunting. McLeod was also a man of firm principles and personal courage. A prominent figure in the fishing industry, he spoke out publicly against paua poachers, with the result that large holes were drilled in his boat to sink it at its mooring.

True to form, Willie quickly established himself as the best crew member Don McLeod, not an easy man to impress, had ever had. When he went off for his spells with the Territorials and McLeod had to take on someone else temporarily, he was always impatient for Willie to get back. Don's partner, Karen Manos, could clearly see the two were cut from the same cloth. But she also noted that they never had a fight, which is almost unheard of for two alpha males.

The boat on which Don and Willie worked was called *Miss Jade*. After McLeod died it was sold and then sold again. It is now owned by Dave Woods.

I had an awesome relationship with Don. He was so down-to-earth. He was a professional jet-boat racer, a national champ who also did jet-boat racing in the United States. When he was out on the water in the fishing boat, you would swear it was the jet boat he was driving.

I had the utmost respect for him. Especially when we were fishing. We only worked when the sea was good enough for us to set lines, and the wind was in a good state. The money was good. We used to do 100 days for the season, heading out every day that the sea would let us, and we would make over $30,000 in 100 days.

We had a fishing base that we used to go back to again and again. But we would always go to a slightly different spot in the area, and every time we would come back around again it was replenished.

You had to be on your toes. It was just him and me. One day we had to chop the line in half because of sharks. There were about 300 sharks that day. We had to bring in what we had on the boat, pick up the rest of the line and get out of there.

I've been on some fishing boats that stink, and there's nothing worse than a stinking boat. When I used to step off our boat, it was always clean. You don't stop working until you've finished all your gear – got the lines all packed away and the fish all gutted and clean and the boat scrubbed down. It's gears before beers, just like in the Army.

If Don hadn't died in a car crash, I'd probably still be fishing. It was a freak accident. He took his eyes off the road and when he looked back up he corrected himself, but the car rolled on the straight and he broke his neck.

CHAPTER SEVEN

TRAVELLER

'Who are those guys?' Willie asked a TF mate. Without knowing many details, they had been assigned to assist on a course, and this was day one.

'They're the SAS.'

'Who are the SAS?'

And then the stories started to pour out, the kind of legendary horror stories that are familiar to anyone who has heard about the SAS but doesn't really know anything about them.

Willie and his comrades were to play the enemy on a tracking course the SAS was running for badged members who had made it through the Group's selection process and 'cycle' – the nine-month training programme that culminates in badging, when a soldier receives the simple beret and belt that mark his status as a fully fledged SAS member.

The 1st New Zealand Special Air Service Group was formed in 1955 in response to a request from the British government for assistance with operations in Malaya. It was placed under the command of Major Frank Rennie, for whom its Papakura base is named, and began training at Waiouru. It served with distinction in Malaya, Borneo and numerous other theatres, acquiring a reputation as a discreet organisation, although there have been widely varying degrees of discretion over the years. In 1955, for example, the SAS contingent marched through Wellington led by Frank Rennie on a farewell parade before leaving for Malaya. More recently, in the interests of efficiency, and to improve their ability to get the job done, the SAS has erred on the side of discretion. Details of their operations – if any – are not made known. Likewise, members are not allowed to be publicly identified. In years to come, the actions of Willie Apiata would modify that policy somewhat.

After the Vietnam War ended, it would be more than two decades before the SAS saw active duty again. However, Vietnam veterans kept the SAS standards and operational capacity alive. Even though many who passed through the unit in those years would never get to use their skills operationally, they acquired them, maintained them, and passed them on to the next generation. Today's SAS owes those anonymous and unsung men a huge debt. Without them it would not exist.

But Willie, who would become the NZSAS's best known member, was unaware the SAS existed until he was assigned to work with them. After hearing his first description of them, he might have expected a bunch of stiff-backed tough guys. Instead, he met a friendly group of relaxed professionals. They were fit, well built and oozed professionalism from every pore. The SAS sets little store by such traditional military markers as hair length and snappy salutes. Some of the men had long shaggy hair, while that of others was neatly trimmed. But they all had one thing in common – each man personified the qualities Willie most admired.

Although he watched what he said around them, in case he inadvertently uttered something that would invite disembowelment, Willie found the reality far different from the SAS legend. He never once saw anyone hung from a tree by his testicles. When they walked, their knuckles remained high above the ground. And if there was any chickens' blood being drunk, no one offered him any. All he saw was normal men, going about their business. He was in awe, he was hooked, and he wanted to join.

With this exercise, too, he witnessed the Group doing what they do best. New Zealand SAS members came into their own as trackers during the Malayan emergency. Now the unit's tracking abilities are regarded as second to none, and their expertise is frequently sought out by their overseas equivalents. Foreign soldiers are often to be found on New Zealand training courses.

Willie's role on the exercise was to be the quarry for what in real life would have been a deadly game of hide-and-seek. Although he was there only as an extra, playing the small part of a gunner in the scenario created for the men on course, he took the opportunity to learn everything he could along the way.

Tracking is tuning in to what's around you. It's a lot like hunting. When you come across signs of a pig, like its footprints, first you judge its size, then the age, how many pigs there are, and where they are heading. The footprints may be fresh or getting old. You might find faeces that's still warm. And if you know the area well, because you have hunted there before, you can work out more than that. After you've done a bit of this, you develop a sense that lets you work out what you need to know quite quickly.

In a way, good tracking is the combination of a lot of skills people don't realise they already have. Take a field on a frosty morning – if someone has walked across it, you can tell things like which way they are going from the colour of the grass. Where the grass has been flattened, the colour will be dull, because it has been walked on. The way the grass is pointing tells you which way the person is walking.

We learnt about covering tracks, too. In the snow, you brush over where you've walked. And in the bush, when you've walked through a place and pushed the grass over, you turn around and push it back the other way after you've gone through. It's like opening and closing a gate. Although some-times you can leave more signs trying to cover your tracks than you made in the first place.

At one point on the exercise, the Directing Staff with us, a badged guy, said, 'I want you to stay here and ambush these guys.' I saw these dudes coming, and it was the first time I'd seen anything like it. It was so professional, the way they came over the rise and scanned the area, looking for signs of us, trying to see where our tracks were heading. And they could see it because they had prepared themselves.

Our primary purpose was to lay tracks and leave footprints for them to find and follow in the bush. We started off with short tracks, but the main exercise was a long one which took over a week. We would go half a day or a day ahead, and they had to interpret where we were heading, how many of us there were and gather as much information from our tracks as they could.

We got to sit in on the presentation at the end of the course, and we saw how much information they had gathered and what they found. It was incredible. For instance, they knew I was the gunner in the group, because they picked up how my gun was always resting; and that because we were on the run, I was always watching the rear. And because it was my first time doing anything like this, I'd been stubbing my cigarettes out in the ground and hiding them as we went along, but they saw the indentations. In the presentation, they produced a plastic bag full of my cigarette butts.

I couldn't believe what they did then, but now I'm a tracker, I totally understand. They can see things where someone who isn't trained could be looking for ages and never see anything. And they can tell a whole story from it.

Another good thing about it was that we weren't just the enemy party, sitting in the bush waiting to go and lay our next track. They set up jungle lanes and observation stands for us. And we got to interact with them.

I did about three of those courses, and each time I came up against different members from the unit. There would be the odd one who would tell you some good war stories around the campfire, and I would be hanging on every word.

It cemented my desire to one day come up to do selection. That planted the seed, no doubt about that, and then it grew, and grew and grew.

Willie had a lot more time to serve in the TF before he would attempt selection for the SAS. His stint included three trips to Australia for exercises.

The first was to Townsville and would always be fondly remembered by him because it included a large amount of live firing. There was patrolling on foot, riding in armoured personnel carriers – ultimate fun for a self-described petrol head – and advancing to contact; contact being the comfortingly bland description for actually engaging in battle with an enemy.

Work hard, play hard and gears before beers. The trip finished with R and R. The men had been warned to avoid some of the bars in town because they did not welcome military. So they started with those.

Their last stop was the Multicultural Bar, which they had also been warned off. 'Multicultural' meant frequented by Aboriginals. The New Zealanders did a haka, which went down well with the patrons.

On Willie's second trip, the group went as far as they could go, from Cairns to Port Augusta, near Adelaide, at the other end of the country. Willie was much less enthusiastic about this exercise due to the scarcity of live ammunition. He hadn't joined the Army – week-end-only warrior or not – to spend his time running around a desert yelling 'Bullets!' or 'Bang!' whenever he encountered someone playing the enemy in simulated contact. But that is what he was required to do on this occasion.

On the trip, Willie and two others were preparing for the SAS selection course and he decided to add a few extras to his routine to build up his fitness. After one day's exercise he and a mate asked to be dropped off about 10 kilometres before reaching base so he could do some extra pack walking. The platoon commander was also one of those preparing for selection and said he would join the pair. Riding in front and looking ahead, he chose a drop-off point from the map.

It all looked terribly unfamiliar to Willie and his mate, who had noticed a water tank as a landmark in the barren landscape at about 10 kilometres on their way out. According to their maps, nothing was where it should be and there were railway lines where they shouldn't be – unless, of course, they were closer to 20 kilometres from home. Eventually they found the water tank, and a jeep came out to collect them so they would be back before dark and escape discipline for being late.

Again, the R and R was a highlight. The Australians roasted a kangaroo on a spit for the New Zealanders, who reciprocated with a hangi. The soldiers also took full advantage of South Australia's fine wine traditions. The sampling policy at one winery was stretched to its limit, but this was made up for by the high sales volume that resulted.

Willie's mother had a sister, Bonnie, who lived locally, and Willie took the opportunity to catch up with his aunt, inviting her out when the men went to a pub one night. When they got there, however, there was no sign of Willie's mates. He asked after them and was told there was a group of men 'next door'. While wondering where 'next door' could be, Willie saw someone he recognised from another battalion walk out of the men's, get his jacket and go back in again. He followed and discovered a back door through the men's. The stripper was performing on the other side of that. Whipped cream was involved.

Willie went back into the almost deserted bar. 'Let's just have a beer and then we'll go home, Aunty,' he said.

Some of Willie's comrades were welcomed back to his aunt's to stay that night, and the next day he decided to have his first ever round of golf. He rigged up a chilly bin on a set of wheels, filled it with refreshments and rolled it around the course with them. Bonnie had a boil-up ready when they got back.

As a golfer, Willie made a fine rugby player. He achieved some impressive distances, but his accuracy left a lot to be desired. Even when putting. No matter, the round made up in entertainment value what it lacked in golfing quality.

On my second trip to Australia with the TF, my hair was a bit long, and before the trip our platoon commander said, 'I want that hair gone by the morning.' So I turned up the next morning with a shaved head. I was like a light bulb. He was inspecting us and saw me and said, 'Holy —.' I said, 'You wanted the hair gone by the morning, sir.'

On my third and final trip we went to Brisbane and were employed as the Infantry support section and our job was to carry the machine guns and set them up. It takes three guys to operate one.

They couldn't employ us at all, really, so we ended up becoming a section of our own without much to do that was worth doing. They turned us into their own MASH 4077th. We'd only been there three days and we were bored.

We got stuck looking after all the guys who were falling over from the heat. It was annoying, because we so badly wanted to be out there doing something. These fellas who were supposed to be patrolling on the road were falling down and we would be going, 'Pussies! Harden up.'

'Have you had anything to eat today?' I asked one who was looking shattered.

'I had a packet of M&Ms,' he said.

I wasn't impressed. I made him something to eat and then watched him to make sure he ate it.

We were getting probed every night by the Aussies, as part of the exercise. They would come in and fire a shot at the camp, keeping us awake.

When the dudes started probing us, someone suggested we ambush them, and we were right into that, even though we weren't supposed to leave our positions under any circumstances.

We ambushed them at their vehicle, and then they started chasing us down the road because they were annoyed.

I came up against another platoon and stopped because I knew it was our boys. They gave us the normal sentry stuff: 'Advance and be recognised.' I got the classic 'Put your weapon down!' It was pitch black but I put it on the ground, gave him the password and cruised on in.

The platoon commander came out and wanted to know what we had been doing.

'We've been up the road chasing those Aussies,' I said, 'so I think we'll be in a bit of trouble in the morning.'

'So what do you think we should do here, Private?' he said. 'We could tie you to the tree for the moment and let the mozzies have a good go at you, or you could go back to your harbour with your tail between your legs.'

'Tail between my legs sounds fine, sir.'

I walked back. My rifle was still where I had left it on the ground. It took me about 20 minutes to find the thing because it was so dark and it was a good 10 to 15 metres away from me. I stumbled around and eventually managed to find it and got back into my own harbour without getting shot at or causing a disturbance.

The following morning, the sergeant major dealt to us for breaking the rules.

'I don't want to see that rubbish again,' he growled.

He was a hard case, but after that they finally found something for us to do. We weren't the dogsbodies any more, which is what we were sick of. We were made into a heavy weapons section, so we got employed in attacks.

In the end, I learned a lot. I'm a grunt, an infantry guy, and I was learning the Support Fire role. SF means things like how to put a gun in the proper position so that it is used to best effect. When we go to an area, they give us a feature to identify and tell us to mount the machine gun on its tripod in that area. We look at the ground to see where the best place to put the gun is and then mark it in case we have to move so we know where to put it again if we came back.

We will lay numerous targets and record the bearing, distance and target number for each and whether we have fired on them or not. Everything is written on a card so you can target what you have been authorised to lay onto.

In the end, despite the rough start, I was happy with that exercise because I came away with a lot more knowledge than when I began.

Anyone in the New Zealand Armed Forces can apply to become a member of the SAS. Admission is in three stages.

The first stage is a short pre-selection process to make sure the candidate is not wasting his and everyone else's time.

This is followed by the nine-day selection course, the mere description of which is enough to put many people off. It makes Willie's experience when he was confined to barracks during his Territorials training look about as punishing as an afternoon's pig hunting. Eighty candidates at the start and six left standing at the finish is not unusual.

And finally, there is nine months of cycle, which provides training in various aspects of the Group's work. Candidates can drop – or fall – out at any of these three stages, or even later.

Willie attempted selection in 1996, but before he would be allowed to do that, he had to go through pre-selection. It weeds out the over-exuberant who, in the long term, for all their strength and stamina, are not what the SAS want. It also makes sure candidates have the necessary navigational skills, and includes some initiative testing.

As part of Willie's pre-selection, he had to do a time trial. He sprinted all the way to the end, recorded a world-beating time and completely knackered himself. As he sat pouring water over his head he realised it was counterproductive to run himself into the ground.

At Limestone Downs near Port Waikato, there was navigation testing, followed by a swimming test and leadership and problem-solving exercises. The latter involved having a certain number of pieces of timber and needing to get across a minefield by arranging the timber in the right way.

When he reached one checkpoint, Willie – identified as Zero One because his name is at the start of the alphabet; Willie is always first for everything – took the straight-line option and climbed over a fence instead of using a gate as he had been told to. The Directing Staff appeared not to notice that Willie was not keeping strictly to the rules.

'Zero One.' He checked Willie off. 'Go over there and wait.'

Willie sat down. The next candidate to get home had seen him and presumed he could jump over the fence too. This time the DS was not so amenable and stopped him halfway.

'What do you think you're doing?' he growled. 'Get off that fence and give me 20.'

While he was doing the press-ups, the DS realised the offending candidate was not the first to have leapt the fence.

'You too, Zero One. Give me 20.' After what he had just been putting himself through to record a good time, Willie's 20 were doubly hard to get out. But nowhere near as hard as selection itself.

CHAPTER EIGHT

PEACEKEEPER

Selection is testing in many ways. Not least for Willie, it would mean nine days of being starved, with candidates supplied only meagre rations and left to their own devices. If they can keep going, they keep going. If they can't, they go home. And if they are unable to motivate themselves to that point, then they are not going to be any use to the SAS anyway. That's why there are no sergeants screaming at candidates and shouting orders in the unit. They either do it or they don't. Whilst the Group would like every candidate to pass, they will only take those who are good enough and if that means that nobody passes then so be it.

Willie received great support from his Territorial Force unit, 6 Hauraki, based in Tauranga, when he went for selection. The

TF loves nothing better than for their recruits to get through. It obviously reflects well on the training they have received in the Territorials. His unit issued Willie the gear he needed, such as maps of areas he was training in, and helped him with training itself. George came out now and then to see how he was doing and assess his fitness level. He put Willie through a few paces and let him know some of the things to expect when he got to the second period and actual selection.

The key to getting through, everyone said, is wanting it enough. If you really, really want to make selection, then you will. Dilettantes are neither encouraged nor enabled. The only thing that can stop a person is not having prepared himself, physically and – possibly even more importantly – mentally.

Willie lasted about 15 minutes. He was out on the first day.

Thanks to his training, his legs were incredibly fit. He could walk for miles, and carry his navigation gear without difficulty. Although it was not his best skill, his navigational abilities were good enough to allow him to read the ground and get from A to B successfully. But he had injured himself not long before. He had been pruning and fell 10 metres out of one tree and landed on another. He hit his shoulder, and it had not been healed for long when he came up for selection.

He had managed the pack walking and other carrying all right. Admittedly, he had fudged somewhat by letting his back take more weight than it should have, because he did not have the real strength he needed in his shoulders. Then the men had to do 30 press-ups, and Willie could barely manage 28. He needed only two more to be able to carry on, but he just couldn't squeeze them out. For someone of his height, press-ups present an often overlooked problem – he has further to press because his arms are longer. He regarded with some envy shorter people who were at an advantage because they did not have to carry their own weight so far. After press-up number 28, Willie returned to the barracks for a shower, got changed and went up before the Training Officer. He had a brief interview and that was it. He was on the bus, heading home, thoroughly gutted.

Everyone back at 6 Hauraki congratulated him for going up and having a go. Everyone knew it took courage for a man to try out for the SAS. It meant he had put his hand up and said: 'I think I've got what it takes.'

'Don't worry about it,' they told him. 'Just get back on and do some more training – there'll always be another chance.' Willie knew he would indeed have another chance, but he was not sure when.

Before he could attempt selection a second time, he was to gain some experience as a 'real' soldier. He wouldn't be running up to people and shouting 'Bullets', or making lights blink on laser vests this time. Instead, he would be part of a deployment of peacekeeping troops from New Zealand as one of 17 countries providing personnel for the United Nations International Force for East Timor, following that country's 1999 vote for independence from Indonesia.

By this time he had stopped fishing with Don McLeod. The work had always been casual and weather-dependent. Willie needed to keep working, and during a lull he took on a job for a security firm that turned out to be not such a good choice. In fact, things in general started looking dismal. It was during this period that McLeod died, and with the security work not proving enjoyable, Willie decided to ring George to see what he might be able to do. He had an inkling there could be something interesting on the horizon.

Troops had already been assigned for the East Timor deployment, and Willie's name was not among them. Training had been going on for two weeks, and his old staff sergeant had been trying unsuccessfully to get hold of him, ringing not just Willie, but friends and friends of friends – anyone who might conceivably hear from him. He knew Willie would be an asset and was keen to have him there. Eventually, someone left a message on the right phone and Willie rang in.

'I just got the message – can I get on the trip?' pleaded Willie.

'You're putting me on the line here,' George told him. Even though he was determined Willie would go, he wasn't necessarily going to make it easy for him. 'I'll tell you what – I'll put your name down, but you have to turn up here tomorrow morning for an RFL.'

Willie didn't stop to think, or do anything else. He jumped straight in his car and drove through the night from Wellington to Tauranga, where he showed he had the Required Fitness Level, even without any sleep.

At the end of the preliminary training, Willie's food-providing instincts kicked in, and he offered to make the most of his fishing contacts to organise some seafood for his group. He went to Wellington and came back with boxes full of salmon and live crayfish, and a bag of mussels, which went down well, variously battered, fried and raw.

He would be with 6 Hauraki Battalion on the third rotation of soldiers to go to East Timor. His family saw him off in fine style. The number of things in the bag he was given to hang around his neck began to look like it was going to weigh more than his pack. The little pouch contained, among other things, paua shell, greenstone, and sand from the beach where the children used to play. There was some hair; a fingernail; a small piece of driftwood from 'their' river with string threaded through it; a scarf with everyone's names written on it. As departure drew closer, more and more items would be found that had to go in the bag.

When he was safely away, Willie, who was a good letter writer

– not only to family but to old friends such as McLeod's bereaved partner, Karen Manos – would write home and explain that he could only wear one or two things at a time, because he didn't want to risk injury by wearing them all at once. He must have looked after them well, because he has all those items to this day.

I was in East Timor for six months. It wasn't passing through on a flying visit like the Australian exercises. It was fantastic to see how the people lived. They recycle everything from their gardens and their animals. They soon learnt how to relate to us. One thing I like doing wherever I go is trying the local food. They had watermelons, mangoes, pineapples and coconuts. There was a mango tree right outside the lines.

The kids would come to the compound fences and say, 'Kia ora, Kiwis' or, 'Wassup?' We would give them chocolate bars through the wire and ask them to get us a coconut. They would go straight up the nearest tree, it didn't matter how high it was, and shin up and get us one.

We had to ask the kids to go because we got banned from climbing the coconut trees. One of our boys had a tomahawk that he used to chop footholds into a coconut tree and climb up. At the top he grabbed a dead frond to hold on to, but it came down and brought a bees' nest with it. All these bees attached themselves to his head and he ended up with about 50 stings. His arms were raw with them, and he was all swollen up. He hadn't been allergic to bee stings before, but he was now.

We were there as reconnaissance. Our job was to go out on patrols and report on any movement we found. If there was critical information, you got on the radio and sent it back. But you weren't allowed to get involved, so it was like you had to pretend you weren't there, or you were invisible. You were like a human CCTV.

We spent the first two weeks in the country getting acclimatised, practising our drills and getting used to our weapons. We had to know where the bases the Kiwis were supporting were. It seemed to take forever before we got out in the field. Then we did the handover with the previous recon team, who briefed us on what they had done and learnt. After that it was up to us.

We had a sighting on our very first patrol. An individual carrying a shotgun walked right into us, but he wasn't aiming it at us. Our rules of engagement were that you could only shoot someone if your life was in danger. He could have been a hunter, but the fact he was sighted going over the border the very next day confirmed he was militia. I had thought we would have to go a long way before bumping into anyone like that, but we were not very far from our base.

It was a rush, but it was our job to get in and get out without anyone even knowing. And we were never compromised again after that first time. That was day one, and it was the only encounter we had during our tour.

There was one other time when we were in position and could see Indonesian soldiers across the border, on a range where their camps were. We spent some time watching them, working out what their routines were and reporting back. One of our guys was an awesome artist who could sketch anything. He did a brilliant five-page panoramic sketch of the whole range that we took back to intelligence. We didn't have digital or any other sort of cameras. Everything we saw we either sketched or wrote down a description of or remembered.

The Reconnaissance are the infantry elite. You have to be disciplined in your soldier skills and how you conduct yourself in the bush. Only certain people can do it. It's not easy to spend two weeks out there sitting on your bum or crawling around on your hands and knees in a tiny space, waiting for someone to appear. When you've finished your patrol, you put your pack back on, and it's a lot lighter because you've gone through all your kai. And you're drained. You're fit and good to go when you go in there, but after two weeks of little or no movement you're stuffed. Part of the discipline we learn in the SAS is being able to keep going after a period like that no matter how fatigued you are.

One day we were patrolling and when we stopped for a break we could hear people talking. Then we could hear them walking. There was a little track below us, but because of the bush you couldn't see much. Then we saw the tops of these little black heads coming along. Our reflexes were all set to go, and we were ready for a major scrap. Then we realised it was a line of wild pigs. The heads were their bristles and the talking was them grunting.

There were rats everywhere, too. There wasn't much you could do about them when you were out. When you are asleep, they will run across your body, and occasionally one stops for a nibble because they think you're quite tasty. You only need to move and they roll off, but one night I could feel something on my face and realised it was a rat chewing my moustache. They would also chew into our packs. We had to put our rubbish in them, because we couldn't leave anything behind, and the rats would go after it. We tried to make snares with what we had out there, but it was a losing battle.

There were plenty of snakes, most of them small, but some very poisonous ones. A mate stood on one without realising it once and it sunk its fangs into his boot. We were out and couldn't make any noise, so he was standing there with his mouth a mile wide, doing a silent scream.

Another time, it was raining and I was having a nap in my hootchie when a mate shook me awake. He pointed and I saw a snake had crawled in under me and gone to sleep where it was dry and warm. I killed it with a rock.

'Have you ever eaten snake before?' I asked him, before cooking it up right there and then. It was hard to skin but all right chopped up like tuna. It was a non-poisonous one, obviously.

Then there were the wasps, scorpions and mosquitoes. But the way I saw it, the bugs were there first. We were in their home. There is nothing to worry about from creatures like that if you prepare your ground properly first, and we are shown how to do that. Malaria and dengue fever are a risk, but for-tunately the insect repellent we're given is extremely grunty. It will take the plastic off a watch if it's not a heavy-duty one.

Now there are proper buildings there, but in my day the lines were tents. We called them Walser lines after Tony Walser who tragically died in a vehicle accident. We 'borrowed' some timber from the engineers after dark one night to fix them up, because they were falling down around our ears. We'd asked if there was any timber we could have and had been told there wasn't. So when we found some that looked like what we wanted, we felt entitled to help ourselves.

The engineers came over and saw the struts we had up. By that time everything was pretty much hammered on and there wasn't a lot they could pick up and take away again.

'I believe you guys were spotted last night ripping timber from over at our compound,' said one.

'Yeah, why is that?'

'There's some timber missing. All we want is if you could please bring it back.'

There was nothing we could do about the timber we'd already used up, but we gave back all the offcuts.

In the middle of it all, there are always some fun days arranged for the troop to keep up morale. We had a theme day and our platoon dressed up as cavemen. Another time, a mate and I hired a boat and taught ourselves to water ski really quickly. We water skied to Dili and back. We went to a place that had been a resort until it was burnt to the ground. But the wharf and the coral reefs were still there. We had a great day at that spot.

Also in East Timor at this time were some members of the SAS. One, who would be with Willie in Afghanistan years later, on the night he performed the deed that won him the Victoria Cross, noticed the young soldier partly for his enthusiasm but mainly because of his size and affable personality. Willie was and is the sort of man who will always be the first to introduce himself, sit down and have a yarn with anyone.

But the most important contact during that half-year was with his family. Systems for communicating with the folks back home are a lot better than they used to be, and those in New Zealand and East Timor made the most of them. There were regular phone calls to his mum, partner and his sisters. Willie would get long letters and packages with magazines and drawings to entertain him. His mum and partner kept him supplied with tinned lamb's tongues and corned beef – his inevitable requests when anyone asked him if there was anything he wanted them to send.

Willie's mum had been very concerned when he first went overseas, not really knowing what was involved or what to expect. A New Zealand soldier, Leonard Manning, had been killed not long before Willie's rotation. The events in East Timor were in the news constantly so were hard to ignore. The family learned the difference between watching an event on television that only concerns other people and following one which involves someone you love. Despite the relatively low risk, it was a great relief when Willie finally arrived safely home at the end of his six-month stint.

Some expected that given how much he had enjoyed the experience he might go into the Regular Force, but he was disinclined. At heart, his real goal was selection for the SAS. In the meantime, civilian life still had its pleasures. He and his partner moved to Whakatane and he found himself settling comfortably into provincial town life. He got a job delivering bread.

CHAPTER NINE

INSIDER

The thrills afforded by a Bay of Plenty bread run were only going to hold Willie's interest for so long. Because the job was new, he enjoyed it at first, but once he'd worked out how to do it and established a routine, that is what it became: routine. Every day was the same.

Although he did like the doughnuts and fresh mince and cheese pies every morning, and although even his dogs were living on pies, doughnuts and their choice of garlic or herb bread, it wasn't enough. Not even the fun of bartering with other suppliers to swap some bread for, say, milk and cheese was sufficient. So he resorted to inventing challenges for himself on his shifts: how many trays of bread could he put on his trolley and get down the ramp in one hit? How many could he carry at once? Despite these efforts, after a couple of months he hit the wall.

One day the phone rang and it was a former SAS member he had met in the Territorial Force. Prior to East Timor, Ray had taken him on pre-deployment training with George, notably the reconnaissance patrol procedures that Willie loved.

'Are you still coming up to do selection again?' inquired Ray.

It was the nudge Willie needed. Without a moment's hesitation he said yes.

'Maybe I'll send you a training programme, and you can give me a call if you need a hand.'

'Sweet, bro.'

Willie had worked hard before, taking on big challenges, setting himself goals and achieving them. But there had been few disappointments to equal missing out on selection because he couldn't manage two extra press-ups, and this time he was taking no chances. He threw himself into a training programme that bordered on the superhuman.

Keeping strictly to the regime, even when still doing his bread run, he'd get up at midnight to start the job, then do his training and finish at three in the afternoon. Depending on his work commitments he would train straight after his shifts. The programme included gym work, pool work, regular running, boot running and track walking. He would train five days a week, but preferably six, with just one rest day. At some points in the training he had to do 15- and then 30-kilometre walks. Such walks inevitably consume large amounts of time. Even the fittest person cannot squeeze them into half an hour, and as a result Willie might finish training at seven or eight at night when he had to be up again at midnight for work.

He rang his adviser.

'I'm feeling absolutely shagged. I'm training my butt off and working, and I think I've hit the wall.'

'Cut it back a bit,' recommended Ray. 'Take a couple of days off and don't do anything and then get back into it.'

Willie began to see the value of pacing himself. It was a lesson he would be glad to have learnt once he was in the middle of selection.

There were people around Willie ready and willing to help or even join him. But with Willie setting a pace pitched at his own tougher-than-average level, the mate who started to train with him soon pulled out. However, Willie would still drive from Whakatane to Rotorua to do pool work with him. At other times, he would drive to Tauranga, where a cousin who was a kick boxer and had his own gym developed a personalised kick-boxing programme for the would-be SAS member. Even Willie's boss at the bakery wanted to get in on the act. Observing how fit his driver was getting, he asked if he could work out with him. He came once and didn't ask for a return engagement, although he was stunned that Willie could do a full day's work along with such demanding training.

The routine was maintained until the very day before Willie left for selection. He cut right back then because he knew he was fit – and he knew that he needed to peak during selection, not the day before. He also took to heart a piece of tactical advice: he did not need to be the fastest at everything. People who were fastest at everything never stayed fast for long. They would burn out early, while those who managed a steady pace could keep going a lot longer. To get through selection, you needed to be able to keep going for a very long time.

If the maximum time for the Required Fitness Level standard was 10 minutes, then it made sense to do it in nine. You didn't get extra points for doing it in eight. Likewise, a good place to finish a Basic Fitness Test is with the rest of the group, not ahead on your own, breaking a record, when you have a lot of other things to do later in the day. At the same time, it would be important for Willie to remember that time spent resting at a checkpoint counted as part of his total. If you spent five minutes at each of five checkpoints, you added 25 minutes to your total time; 10 minutes each and you added nearly an hour. It was a bit like chess, with lots of little things that could make a big difference to think about. And on selection, the day isn't finished until someone tells you it's finished. One of the big psychological challenges of the process is that those taking part can't be sure when any given exercise will be over. There may still be a swim test and a spot of sleep deprivation before the following day's cross-country walk.

Willie already knew a little about what would be involved, but not everything. He had, of course, heard all the stories from those who had been through it – or partway through it – but there was no guarantee that his course would be like theirs. He knew he had to do navigation early on, as well as some sort of cross-country exercise, plus a 60-kilometre walk at the end. But he had no idea what to expect in between. And it wouldn't be entirely beyond the bounds of possibility for the SAS to change the rules at the last minute. Consequently, Willie the good protégé picked the brains of every mentor he could find – both those who had done selection and those who hadn't made it.

Some people prepared themselves for selection with a diet of KFC and a few games of tennis. That wouldn't have improved their chances much, but it didn't necessarily mean they would miss out. Willie chose the approach that looked likely to get the best results. He wanted not just to pass but to pass well. But there is no guaranteed way of getting through. Even though he would seem to have the ideal physique for the job, all sorts of shapes and sizes make it.

Appearances can be deceptive. Some very average-looking men have made it through selection, and SAS members have given up trying to predict on day one who will or will not be there at the end.

The only thing anyone knows for sure is that the ultimate factor determining a candidate's success is how badly they want it. As one mentor told him: 'When the will is strong, everything else is easy.' And Willie's will to win surpassed everything else. Just as with many SAS activities, it took the mental side of things to enable the physical side to happen. If his body hit the wall, his mind would not agree with it. Not that his body was likely to let him down at this point, but his mind would carry him through.

One of the keys to success may be not questioning what you're asked to do. A couple of officers were on the pre-selection Willie had to do before his second selection attempt. One was a South African former Special Forces soldier who was loud and long in his descriptions of how well he was going to do. Willie got a nudge from one of his mates. 'There's no way this guy will make it through selection,' he said. And he was right. This guy didn't even make it *to* selection. Early on he started complaining about what he was being asked to do because he didn't see the point of it. 'Why are we walking up these hills?' he grizzled. 'I didn't come here to do this – I came here to be selected.' Apparently, he believed his position as an officer conferred him special status – a view directly contradictory to the SAS's egalitarian, all-in-this-together ethos.

Having already missed out once, Willie knew he would finish selection the second time, no matter what. It would take a broken leg to stop him this time – and even then, it would have to be a very bad break. Some people, though, don't even make it through the initial fitness test. One candidate in Willie's group had already run out of water at this point. Someone refilled his bottle, but he swallowed the lot and immediately brought it back up. Everyone could tell he wasn't going to last much longer. The next day, during the navigation exercise, he was badly dehydrated and only made it to the second checkpoint before being told he was out.

The navigation exercise is the second component of selection. Navigation, after all, is one of the core SAS skills, and some aptitude is essential. Willie was well equipped for navigation, not least because he had always taken an interest in it and had done something similar on his first pre-selection. He knew, for instance, to examine the ranges he would be covering and look for routes that would be easier and less demanding, if longer, rather than shorter but steeper and draining. As long as you finished within the allotted time, it was better to conserve energy by going a little slower and further, rather than risk burning yourself out over a more direct but harder route.

The men were loaded into a truck that dropped them off with a grid and left them to find their way to the next checkpoint. Not that it all went perfectly. At one point Willie was nearly run over by geese as he was trying to cross a creek. But he wasn't so startled that he didn't realise that where there were geese, there would be food.

Foraging around the banks of the creek, he turned up a nest full of eggs hidden away in a bush. He took them down to the water and put them in to see which floated and which sank, so he would know if any were fresh. When he found one that sank, he tucked it in a pocket, returned the other eggs to the nest and headed to the next checkpoint. He was making such good time he thought he could afford to stop for a snack. Finding a secure spot in the bush, he knocked the top off the egg. For someone who has eaten so many eggs, and had experience of such a wide variety of them, it was a genuine novelty to encounter something that tasted quite this bad.

He vomited the egg straight back up and threw the rest away.

One part of selection that usually marks the end of the road for several candidates is an exercise that involves carrying jerry cans for 20 hours. Supervisors take a day and night shift to oversee it. Sometimes it is done through swamp, but Willie's group had to do it over sand dunes. Neither option is easier than the other. At the time, he thought the jerry can-carrying drill was a bit of unnecessary torture, but has since found himself having to do it on a real procedure. The SAS isn't the sort of organisation to indulge in pointless activities.

We went to the dunes with about 12 people left because so many drop out in navigation. You would never know until the evening who had made it through to the next day. At parade there were always fewer people present than there had been the night before. And it was like they had never been there at all. Those who make it through the dunes – or swamp – have a good chance of finishing. But a lot have decided by now this is not for them.

It was important to conserve your energy doing the dunes. You had some guys that picked up their jerry cans and away they went. But you knew you were in there for 20 hours, so you had to go at a pace that was acceptable. You just did it. On the close country, the next stage after the dunes, you are effectively walking to the start of the 60-kilometre walk, which is the last thing you do in selection – and the last thing you feel like doing. You probably start 50 kilometres from there and have to hit the checkpoints again. You've got to walk a long way and you have two to three days to do it.

I was keen to get started because I had a plan. Whether it's the open country or the close country part of selection, there's no using the roads. If you get caught on the road, you get taken back so many kilometres to start again. I thought if I made the first three checkpoints early, then maybe the next day I could cut back a bit and save some energy for the 60 kilometres.

I went hard to every single checkpoint. When I got to the second, one of the staff was there.

'You haven't got much time, but if you make it to the next one, there may be a surprise waiting for you,' he said.

My eyes lit up and that was it. I dived back into the bush.

I got to the third checkpoint.

'Zero One, Staff.'

'You're cutting it fine, Apiata. It's just about dark.'

You weren't allowed to carry on if it was dark, but I had made it, and he gave me the next grid. However, something wasn't right – no surprise. But I knew not to question it or say anything at all. I started to walk away.

'Get back here,' he ordered.

I went back.

'Go over to the truck and get a ration pack.'

I was so happy! Grabbing the pack and sprinting into the bush, I put my hootchie up and consumed a whole ration pack just like that.

The next morning was beautiful. The sun was coming up when I woke up. By now I was used to waking with nothing in my stomach, but not today. My time was good, and I was ahead of nearly everybody. I had some muesli and away I went again.

It was about eight kilometres to the next checkpoint, which was heading uphill to a lookout. I got to the area, put down my weapon and got out my map to work out the route and see where I should be going next. It looked to me like I only had another kilometre and a half, maybe two. It was all good. I got up and cruised over to the checkpoint. There was the truck waiting for me, right on time.

'Zero One, Staff!'

'Where's your weapon, Apiata?'

My weapon was sitting where I had left it when I stopped to check the map! Because I was concentrating on going hard out, I'd forgotten to pick it up. My mind exploded.

'Going to get it, Staff!'

I started running although I didn't really know where I was going. I stopped and all I could think was: 'I dropped my weapon!' Plus I was out of water, because I had used it all up getting to the last checkpoint. The only thing that you get lots of on selection is water. It's like petrol in an engine – as long as you keep pouring that into your body and your body is absorbing it, there's nothing that can stop you.

But there was no way I could remember where I'd put my rifle down. I couldn't even remember whether I had it in my hand when I left my hootchie. So that was it – I had to start going all the way back to try to find it.

On the way, I came across the boys, and they thought I'd gone loopy because I had no pack, no weapon – nothing. And I was pale and starting to get dehydrated.

'What's going on, Willie?'

'Bro, have you seen my rifle?'

'What? No.'

'Okay, see you. I gotta go.'

I went back to where I'd sat down, but it wasn't the exact place. I was crashing round in a frenzy and not having any luck. So the only thing for it was to track myself. And that meant covering even more ground, because I had to go back near the beginning and follow my route, rather than walking towards it. If I just walked back towards my starting point, in the opposite direction from how I had come, all the grass would be pointing at me and it would be harder to see. But if I circled round and followed my track, it would be easier, because the grass would be a different colour where I'd trodden it down.

I started tracking my way back on the trot. Along the way, I ran into another group and asked them for a drink. They handed me their water bottle and I downed the lot. Turned out that was their last drink of water too.

As I was running down the road, Staff went past in his four-wheeler, obviously thinking I had lost it. But he also would have been thinking: 'I hope Apiata finds his rifle, because if he doesn't we'll have to.' You can't just leave rifles lying around the countryside.

I finally got back to my hootchie space and looked all around. There was nothing there. I thought I was done. That would be the end of me and selection for the second time. But refusing to give up, I tracked my way back over a dead area that had been logged, following my signs. I got all the way back to where I'd sat down and done my last map check. And there was my rifle! I picked it up and kissed it and promised it I would never let it go again.

Then I started running back to the checkpoint I'd already reached, passing my mates again. I had passed them all, been all the way back, tracked myself back and then passed them again and finally got to the checkpoint. I worked out that I'd probably added 15 kilometres to the amount of ground I had to cover by the time I'd done all the doubling back.

'So you found your rifle? Don't worry about it any more, concentrate on getting to the end.'

'Yes, Staff.'

Getting me some water, he made me have a drink and clean my weapon. Then held me there for half an hour before telling me where the next checkpoint was and letting me get on my way. As soon as he did that, I was sprinting to make up for the lost time. I managed to get to the end that night, and I think I came in third out of all the boys. Then came the 60-kilometre walk.

But before that, Staff said to me: 'What lesson have you learned?'

'Not to leave my weapon behind, Staff.'

'Will you ever do that again?'

'No, Staff.'

'Is this going to haunt you?'

'Yes, Staff.'

And then it was off again. You didn't have to navigate anything on the 60-kilometre section, you just followed the route. Every 10 kilometres or so, they would have someone stationed with a jerry can of water so you could get a refill. I always made sure that by the time I got to the stop I would be just about out of water, because if I wasn't, then it meant I hadn't been drinking enough as I went along.

However, I did something on that last section that I've never been able to do again: I ambled – the way a horse does when it's not on the full trot. It took me about 20 kilometres to get into it, but I ambled the whole way. I never stopped to eat – I had rations in my pouches, so I could tear them open and munch away and keep the rubbish with me. And I passed everyone on the way, even though they had made me start from way back again.

There was a medic waiting at an ambulance at one of the water stops. Because he wasn't badged, I thought I could get some information out of him. I asked him how much further we had to go, because I had no way of telling.

'You know I can't tell you that,' he said, 'or those guys will give me a hiding. But I can tell you this: you'll be seeing me again.'

'Now I'm really depressed,' I said.

I filled up my water bottle and kept going. It was starting to get dark when I came down a road, and sure enough, there was the same medic again. I met some of the boys who were going the opposite way, so they didn't know yet how much further they had to go. They were limping and looked absolutely shattered. I didn't have the heart to tell them they had to go around again.

'Not far to go, not far,' I said.

It was dark when I got to the next checkpoint. I was expecting them to tell me where to go next. But they didn't. It was the finish. They told me to go and get a brew and a ration pack and wait for the others. I think the 60 kilometres took me 10 or 11 hours, and you have to do it in 20. It all takes a while to sink in.

I had been looking forward to selection, and I really enjoyed it. You're truly testing yourself when you take that on.

Willie passed selection. The uncharacteristic absent-mindedness that saw him forget his weapon and have to add several kilometres to an already gruelling exercise could be seen as a blunder, beginner's overexcitement, or a remarkable feat given the way he dealt with it. Most people would plump for the last. Not Willie. Even after he had finished within the allotted time he was convinced the stuff-up with his weapon had ruined his chances.

What he didn't know – and couldn't have known – was that he had already been identified as someone who had just those qualities the SAS seeks in its men. Men like his mentors George and Ray don't encourage someone to apply for the SAS unless they believe that the man and the unit will benefit each other. While such predictions aren't always correct, there's usually a good sense in the first few days of who will make it and who, if anyone, will excel. If Willie hadn't been able to find his gun, he almost certainly would not have passed, but those responsible for denying him admission would have been bitterly disappointed at having to make that decision.

At the end of selection, there's a debrief with the Commanding Officer. No one is standing tall – they're too tired to be capable of it. Feet are sore and almost invariably blistered, muscles and joints are tender. They have had to clean weapons and vehicles, and pack their gear away. No one has had more than a couple of hours' sleep since the end of the course. That fatigue is magnified by the sleep deprivation of the preceding days. Everyone looks gaunt. Willie had gone in at 90 kilos and came out at 85, all his reserves of fat depleted.

Standing there in something of a daze, he listened to what the CO had to say. But he was sure, thanks to his mistake, the news would not be good. The words floated around him until one sentence penetrated his consciousness.

'. . . and I look forward to seeing you when you come back in January to start the cycle.'

Now he believed it. His grin took the ends of his mouth right up to his ears.

Close to 40 men had started, and nine were there at the end. Seven got selected and two left because they didn't meet the criteria in other ways. No one thinks any the less of someone who is not admitted after getting through selection – that in itself is an achievement very few can manage. Even completing cycle is no guarantee of acceptance, as it is only afterwards that some men reveal qualities that make them unsuitable for long-term membership in the Group.

The reduction of 40 candidates to nine could have been a windfall for the survivors because at the start of selection everyone volunteers to put five dollars into a kitty to pay for celebrations at the end. The way they see it is that those left standing are entitled to a beer for getting to the end from those who don't. But the abundant funds went to waste. Everybody's system was so strained and their stomach so shrunken by the end, that when it came time for roistering, it was a case of two beers and lights out. The men were given food in hot boxes because, as big with hunger as their eyes were, their stomachs couldn't handle it all at once, so they put the food away for later.

On his way home from selection, Willie landed at Tauranga airport. As he got off the plane he crossed paths with George, his TF trainer and mentor, who was getting on.

'Hi, Willie – where have you been?'

'On selection.'

'Did you pass?'

'Oh yeah.'

'Choice,' said George, because, having followed Willie's career from the start, it meant almost as much to him as it did to his protégé that he had made it through. And no one's good opinion could have meant more to Willie, because he knew George was the real thing, a man from the old days of the SAS, when the tradition was forged.

CHAPTER TEN

FAST LEARNER

Now Willie was going to be away for nine months doing the SAS training cycle, he had to tell his partner where he had been, and where his life was heading. She picked him up from the airport and as they drove home he explained he had made it through selection.

She was not happy but she knew that there was no mistaking this was Willie's dream. Having found something worth doing, he wasn't going to be able to alter his course for anything. Or anyone. The two were heading into the unknown – Willie didn't even know whether he would get any leave during cycle. (In the event, there were two fortnight-long breaks.) But he quit his job driving the bread truck – his boss wasn't much happier than his partner had been – and began cycle in January 2002.

They say in the SAS that getting selected is hard, finishing cycle and getting badged is harder, and staying in the Group is hardest of all. Willie had been the exception who thrives on the challenges of selection, but it remained to be seen whether he would get through cycle as successfully. For the duration of cycle, and after all the hard work it has taken to get there, no one knows for sure whether or not they have a future in the SAS. They are still being observed and assessed every step of the way.

It is a complex, demanding routine of exercises and lessons designed to equip the candidate with all the skills and resources they may need on an SAS operation. The first three parts include meds (medical work), sigs (signals, or communications), and combat survival. The men also undergo instruction in RTI (resistance to interrogation) and learn CQB (close quarter battle or hand-to-hand fighting). Then there are modules such as Helicopter Co-Operation, Patrol Procedures, Counter Terrorism, Basic Demolitions Handlers, and the Basic Static Line Parachute Course. It all culminates in an exercise called Blue Sabre, where everything that has been learned is put to the test.

There were 10 in Willie's cycle, which completed its counter-terrorism training earlier than usual because some members of the regular CT unit were going overseas and replacements who could take their place if necessary needed to be ready.

Cycle is nothing if not varied. Sigs used to mean learning Morse code and lugging heavy radio equipment around. Modern communications equipment is considerably different, involves satellites and is not necessarily to the taste of someone like Willie, who doesn't find computers particularly congenial. He was disappointed he wasn't going to get to learn the traditional dots and dashes.

Meds was more than first aid and CPR. It was designed to make everyone capable of dealing with injuries in the field and keeping their comrades alive until the real professionals can get to them. It included practice putting drips into each other's arms and was just extreme enough to be enjoyable. No one ever got dehydrated doing meds. The men learnt how to deal with blood trauma, bullet wounds, broken bones, arterial bleeds, drowning and electrocution.

And for a gun enthusiast like Willie, there were exciting new weapons for him to get his hands on. Combat survival, which took place in the bush, Willie's natural element, was his favourite part of cycle. It also featured food prominently at several points, although sometimes the main thing about the food was that there wasn't any.

In the main, he loved everything about cycle. It was hands on, practical and new. It met his needs to learn, and to be active while he was doing so. It was as though every skill he had acquired in his first 30 years was being brought into play but magnified 100 times: roughing it, surviving outside, finding his own food, fearlessness, stamina, gun handling, initiative and teamwork. The possibility that Willie and the SAS were made for each other was confirmed every step of the way.

Combat survival was partly about living off the land. The Directing Staff reminded his pupils of the three things they needed for survival: shelter, water and warmth. Shelter was necessary to protect them from the elements in all sorts of environments; water would keep them alive, because the body cannot do anything without it; and warmth would not only keep them warm but enable them to cook their food if and when they got it. It was essential to have these three basics organised before thinking about finding food. And they were going to learn how to provide all of them for themselves out of nothing.

Their first shelter was constructed out of some old shelters they found, renovating the foundations that were there and recycling sheets of corrugated iron that they placed on top of beams for rafters, before concealing them with ponga fronds placed on top. Instructing them, the Directing Staff, who did not know about the recycled material, told the men that if ponga fronds were laid in the correct manner for a roof, it would be as good as corrugated iron. The men were sure their roof would easily be that good!

Obtaining food meant foraging, in all sorts of ways. The lesson Willie the hunter had to learn was that food from the bush didn't necessarily mean pigs or deer. There was plenty of other food that would get them through. It might not taste very good, but it was still food. The trainees visited a woman with a remarkable knowledge of edible native plants – both well known and obscure – and how to use them, including puha, dandelions and mamaku. Taking them on a tour of her edible garden, she explained the uses of what she grew. While they accepted that eating this stuff could save their lives, no one would be able to persuade them it was delicious. When a salad was prepared for them to sample, they were unanimous that the best part was the dressing.

Of course, if they did find a pig or deer they would be making the most of it. And for that they would need fire. Cooking lessons began with instruction in how to start a fire with flints. You could get a few sparks with flint shavings, magnesium and a knife; and if there was nothing else to start the blaze with, you could use the lint from your pockets.

For an old bushman like Willie, being able to make fire, even in the pouring rain, was the mark of a good hunter. He knew that if you looked in the right places you could always find dry material some-where – it might be dry wood under wet, or it might be the inside of something like ponga which was totally wet on the outside. In the bush you could smoke or grill your food. But if you had a kerosene tin or similar, and could get it hot, you could put a leg of lamb in it and cook a roast in a hole in the ground. Or you could organise an impromptu hangi, without the tin.

All the cooking on combat survival is done without artificial aids, using what you gather in the bush. When the DS opened up the roast he made, it was golden brown. You could see the fat dripping off it and the saliva dripping down our faces. He pulled off a piece of meat and waved it in front of us, saying, 'I'm dying to get into this.'

I remember so many good smells like that. Not just lamb but eels, and chicken wrapped in nikau leaves. You dust off the palm fronds and the dirt and there is a beautiful kai. But for about three days, even though we've been taught how to make a fire to keep us warm, we're not allowed to do any cooking.

They show you how to kill and prepare sheep, rabbits and chickens. A karate chop to the back of a rabbit's neck will do the job quickly and easily if you do it properly. The chickens they had for us to kill and cook were the mangiest old birds I've ever seen. And they talked about drinking the blood, which you can do if you're absolutely desperate, just to survive. But they didn't make us do it. Besides, unless you were going to steal a chicken from somebody's backyard, I don't think you would find too many of them wandering around in the bush waiting to be caught and eaten. But that's where the SAS chicken-strangling and blood-drinking stories come from. I've drunk pig's blood before, though – after all, it's only what black pudding is made out of.

Anyway, we killed a sheep and gutted it, and the DS said he was putting the guts in the stream for eeling and no one was to go near it. We asked if we could do some foraging, though, and he said yes: 'Just stay away from where I'm going eeling.'

We followed behind him while they were eeling and got some eels, including the biggest one that day. The other cycle group caught a little pig and a few small eels. We gutted our eel and hung it up. It had been cleaned in the fire. Then we went for our cooking lessons.

The old guy taking them asked the first group what they had foraged.

'We have mamaku and got us a little pig and a couple of eels.'

'What have you done to your pig?'

'Oh, we singed it, and we smoked it over the fire.'

'Have you had the cooking lesson?'

'No.'

'Then bring the pig down to me. What about your eels?'

'We smoked them over the fire.'

'Bring them down to me.'

So because they went and cooked it before they had had their cooking lesson, all the kai was taken away from them apart from the mamaku. Then he turned to our group.

'What about you?'

'We got some mamaku and an eel.'

'And what have you done to it?'

'We've gutted it.' Which was true. But we didn't say we had smoked it too, so we got to keep ours.

Then we had the lesson. He showed us how to do a cold smoke, a hot smoke, and then a hangi. We were watching and drooling at all the amazing food he managed to prepare. Then we were sent away to do our own.

The food that had been confiscated off the other group had been given back to them, but they had to give half to us. As it turned out, the eels and the pig were flyblown after sitting there for a day but we still ate them. To be fair to all we gave half our big eel to them.

We ate everything we could, but part of the food we foraged we had to save. We wrapped it up in nikau palms and stuffed it into our handmade packs for when we were on the run.

When the men go on the run and are actively pursued for three or four days, they are supplied with next to nothing, but have been taught by now how to make the most of it. Some men on cycle may have come from the Navy or Air Force and have had different background training from the Army men. So it is back to basics for demonstrations. The idea is to make everyone capable – not show up anyone as incapable. Their survival may one day depend on it.

They set off in boots, trousers and thermal top, plus some sacks and parachute material to make clothing and a small tobacco tin-sized container with miscellaneous essentials. Everything they might need – backpack, jacket, hat, gloves, even shelter – has to be created from these plus whatever raw materials they can scavenge from the land. Willie still has everything he made on this exercise.

To begin with he made a backpack out of material he had been given. Then he plaited some rope into two long pieces that he could cut bits off to use as and when required. Everyone had been given a piece of waterproof material about the size of a mattress. It was up to them how they decided to use it. While others cut it up to use for various purposes, such as to line their backpacks, Willie kept his whole and adapted it in all sorts of ingenious ways. For a start, he rolled his other items up in it and then stuffed it in his pack so they were protected from water anyway. You weren't allowed a hootchie on this part of the course, but Willie and a mate thought they could make near enough to one with their material if they used it properly.

'What's this big thing for?' his sergeant demanded when he found the still-whole piece on an inspection.

'I roll all my gear up in there, Staff. Stuff it in there and that's how I keep everything dry.'

'That's a fair and plausible excuse for having that much material in your pack.'

Lying in a ponga frond shelter in the rain at night – without benefit of corrugated iron this time – Willie found himself getting soaked. Getting up, he flicked on his torch and saw two of the others perched like roosters on a fence, holding their tiny cut-down pieces of material over their heads in a vain attempt to keep dry and warm.

'What are you two doing?' he asked.

'We're cold and wet. That guy lied to us – he said it was like corrugated iron.'

Willie lit a fire. He had made himself some twine and used it to stretch out his material for a properly waterproof shelter. The others got as close as they could, although it wasn't big enough for everyone to fit under.

The next morning, it was still raining.

'You fellows are looking pretty wet,' remarked the DS. 'How was your hut?'

'Not as good as Apiata's.'

Inside their small waterproof containers, the men had fishing line, sinkers, Oxo cubes, matches with a waterproof striker, a little torch, a small pocket knife, a compass to orient themselves, needle and thread for sewing up clothes – or themselves – and whatever else they could fit.

One of the things the men have to be prepared for is the high risk of being taken prisoner when on operations. To educate them for this eventuality, among other things, they visited a prison for a small taste of what they might experience if captured. They were shown how prisoners who escaped had managed it, how others had taken the plastic rod that holds a toilet seat to a bowl and sharpened it on concrete to make a weapon – which is why the prison toilets no longer have seats – how a battery could be shorted and used to make enough heat to boil water. Anything and everything could

ABOVE LEFT: NZ Battalion 3 – Six Hauraki lads that were based in Suai.
Note, I have borrowed the SAS guy's weapon.

ABOVE RIGHT: On patrol in Suai local area with NZ Battalion 3.

BELOW: Caveman costume parade, Recon Platoon NZ Battalion 3.

ABOVE: Mobility Troop goes amphibious.

BELOW: Mortar Base Plate training.

ABOVE: Fixing Sexy's vehicle – draining the fuel tank.

ABOVE: Taking the cooling fan out to recover another vehicle – a major mission.

BELOW: What a hairdo! This is what happens when you have been on the motorbike for a few hours as an outrider.

INSET: .50-calibre helicopter sniping.

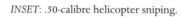

ABOVE: Inspecting captured weapons.

BELOW: Firing the 84-mm Carl Gustav.

ABOVE: A typical Afghan compound.

BELOW: A local goes about his business.

ABOVE: The troop back at base.

BELOW: A small tot of rum and coffee for ANZAC day.

The Squadron.

potentially be of use to someone when doing his job.

On a more cosmic note, they visited the Auckland Observatory for a lesson in how to recognise and navigate by the stars in case they didn't have a compass. After the physically demanding nature of most of cycle, many of the trainees – and Willie was one of them – find this part, lying back and staring at the ceiling in the dark, somewhat sleep-inducing.

But combat survival is probably as close to the real thing as you can get.

We were split into different groups when we went into the bush because there were 10 of us. We had an Officer on ours and when you get through, you are friends for life, no matter what anyone wears on their shoulders. But just because he was the most senior and a good guy didn't mean he was automatically in charge. There were collective decisions to be made. When we were on the run, for example, we had to decide which direction to go in. This was normally done by 'Chinese parliament' where everybody put forward their ideas and we then chose which way to go.

For the exercise you are given a scenario. On our one, it was that a counter-terrorist team was hunting us. Before you start, you get given a password – a number or a day of the week or a month.

There's nothing like being on the run. When we were doing our first one in Coromandel, the cops were doing drug busts, so there was a helicopter flying around plantations which they had sprayed blue. We didn't know whether they would report seeing us. If they did, they would probably think the worst because we only had our basic gear on and could easily have looked like we belonged to the plantations and were on the run from them. Luckily, they left us alone and didn't lead the people pursuing us to where we were.

When you get to a checkpoint, they tell you how long you have to get to the next one. Sometimes he will have information to give you; if not, you keep going and aim to get there as quick as you can.

On our second Combat Survival Module, we had to meet an agent at night. We had a fire going in dense bush, and it was so black you couldn't see your hand. We were in the middle of the bush and had to go a good 300 metres from our fire down to the edge to meet our agent. We did that and got our next co-ordinates and had to make our way back up in the pitch blackness. Even with the fire glowing we couldn't see anything else and it took us ages to find them again.

We had our 'tinfoil' survival blankets over us. One of the others had fallen asleep under his when the helicopters started flying over, trying to find us. They have infrared night sights and the only way we could think of to cover our fire was with the other guy's survival blanket, so we grabbed it and held it on top of the fire. It seemed to be working, but then it burst into flames.

'My blanket – you guys have burnt my blanket!'

'Sorry, bro.'

So that was the end of that. We stamped the fire out. The blankets might even have reflected things back to the helicopter, but we knew there was no way anyone could get up to where we were, even if they had seen us. We'd had a hard enough time getting in there on our own. The best place to sleep is always the worst-looking one, because anyone coming in to get you is going to make a hell of a lot of noise, breaking sticks and tripping over. That's your early warning system.

The next morning, we headed on our way and, sure enough, we found out later that they had come down through the bush to find us, but we were already gone.

When we did the testing on the final one we went so hard that we managed to get in front of all the hunter forces as they were being dropped off, even though we set off a trip flare. Well, the officer set it off, because he was being nosy. We heard him say, 'What's down this track?' and then suddenly a flare went off. We pulled him off the track and dived into the bush, and then all we could hear was the helicopter coming up the valley.

It flew down and was cruising around searching for where we were, and then it flew away. That was a relief. So we kept going and stopped again in a stand of head-high manuka, with a clearing not far away. We had some kai on us and started cooking it up. Mine was just about ready when we heard the helicopter again. It didn't sound like he landed, but he must have, and he must have done it pretty quickly, because the next thing we knew there was a dog on the scene, with its handler and another soldier, and they were so close.

We were lucky that we had a faint breeze blowing on our faces and we didn't walk out into the clearing, so he didn't smell us.

We took off, but didn't really know where we were going.

'Stop, you're taking us into the abyss!' I yelled.

We worked out where we were and where to go and got to some shelter just as it was getting dark, and we had our feed there.

Then we heard more people out there. You learn to recognise people by their shape when you've been working with them, and we realised it was the other cycle group.

One of our group called out, 'Hey, bro,' and their guy shot off. The next one was about to follow him when our guy said, 'Don't run away, it's only us.'

So we had a talk about what we had seen and what had happened to all of us. Then they were on their way again.

When you do the Blue Sabre exercise, you get captured at the end and go through RTI. We didn't get caught, but guys do get caught. If they are, they are taken back and thrown out on the run again.

Towards the end of cycle, I did my Basic Static Line Parachute Course. I didn't like parachuting much, and I still don't. The only jumps I don't mind are water jumps. I'm happy to do it because it's part of my job, but I wouldn't miss it if I didn't have to do it. It's not the falling or the landing that bothers me, it's the time between leaving the aircraft and when the parachute opens. Once I feel the pull of the chute deploying, everything is fine. The team thing is a big part of making it work – you have to jump because there is a man behind you who needs to jump too.

Another part of cycle I found strange at first was close quarter battle. I'm not much of a scrapper, and I've not been in many fights, but in CQB they teach you how to fight. It's all open-hand stuff. You form a circle, they throw you in there and one of your mates comes in. You're not fighting strangers. It's you and your buddies, and there's no holding back. You're trying to learn something, so you're all going hard.

At the start, I was nervous and a little bit scared. When you first step into the circle, it's very intimidating. You've seen guys fight before, and then you get in there, and you're tapping away lightly. Then a guy whacked me in the head, and I got a good one and that was it. You see red. It's either lose or win, not in between. But it's not just you two – you fight every single one of the dudes who are on your side, one after the other, hand-to-hand. If you had any grudges or differences through your cycle, that's where you took it out on each other. Then you're mates afterwards.

We also do it with Pugel sticks – the poles with big pads on that you see on *Gladiators*. We had helmets and gloves and the sticks. After fighting with 10 guys, you're knackered, your arms are shattered, your helmet's vibrating like crazy and you can't see your opponent. But they go hard and expect you to do the same.

Size doesn't make any difference. Big guys, little guys – everyone has to get in there. Four of us were about the same size, but everyone is different in some way, and everyone fights differently. It taught me how to fight, and also how much fight there is in a person and how to control your temper. There's a time and a place for fighting.

It taught me to fight to win. They say you shouldn't box a boxer, or try kung fu on a kung fu fighter. The idea is to take your opponent out as quickly as you can. In the first instance, all you really want to do is get yourself out of there, but if you're backed into a corner and there's no way out, then you have the tools to deal with that. And if that happens, I want to be the guy who's still standing at the end.

We still scrap each other at work today. It's called 'milling'. It may be boxing one day, when we will go in and practise a few moves. Then we'll set up a few mats or make a square or circle, and the boys will get in there with the gloves on and go for it. Later you'll give each other a hard time about it: 'I got you a good one, bro! Did that hurt?'

CQB lasts two weeks. After the hand-to-hand and the staffs, you do pistols, because they are a close quarter combat weapon.

Part of cycle, and part of SAS routine afterward, is the tyre house, also known as the fun house. This is where Method of Entry (MOE) is practised – ways of breaking into a building or any other place, such as a ship, where hostages may be being held. Outside is a pile of spare steel doors, sourced and scavenged from all over, that are used to practise forced entry.

It's an eerie structure, with a flat roof big enough for a helicopter to land on – or to hold the occasional party. Inside it's a maze of almost identical spaces, rendered dark even in daytime because the walls are black tyre. During an exercise, confusion is increased by the noise of holes being blown in concrete or the choking effects of the clouds of smoke pouring through the building. Practice in here is done with live rounds, and it's a skill that must be maintained because no one can afford to be off the boil if they're doing something as high risk as this.

In the near-darkness and amid the deafening noise, traditional commands are not an option. The men communicate by body language as much as anything else. Having worked together so closely in such extreme situations up to this point, one can tell from the turn of a shoulder or the move of a hand what another is going to do. Full-scale enactments of hostage taking and rescue missions attempt to re-create and deal with all possible contingencies. Before breaking in, the troops will have identified their entry point. The aim is to subdue the captors and rescue the hostage.

Everything the SAS uses here they have made themselves, from the explosives to the targets. Judging the right amount of explosive to break through a door is critical.

People who live in the Defence housing near the SAS's MOE house are used to their windows being rattled by helicopters and explosions. However, a far preferable way of practising MOE, from everyone's point of view, is to have a real building to use. For all the ingenuity that goes into making the tyre house a lifelike experience, nothing can equal the real thing. On Willie's cycle, some of the buildings at the Papakura Military Camp were marked for demolition. Who better to carry it out than this enthusiastic bunch?

After anything salvageable had been removed the men demolished the buildings in short order, doing nothing to improve the strokes of those playing golf at a nearby club.

Cycle is punishing. One thing that breaks up the hard work, for a night at least, is the annual regimental dinner. It's a traditional affair, held at Rennie Lines. Sherry before dinner, toasts throughout, and all members of the SAS plus ex Commanding Officers and Regimental Sergeants Major are invited.

There is a guest speaker who tends towards the inspirational: the likes of double-amputee Everest conqueror Mark Inglis, or winning rugby sevens coach Gordon Tietjens. And, after the dignitaries have left, those doing cycle are charged with performing a skit to entertain – if that's the right word – the others. The SAS are not the most patient of audiences, so an inferior act is likely to be quickly drowned out by jeers.

Because Willie had not been in the Regular Army but the Territorials, he didn't have the correct formal dress so could not attend the regimental dinner during his cycle. He was happy to be bartender for the night though.

Willie, on the whole, had a good night. He even made too much money for the group by inadvertently overcharging for the drinks – a fact that came to light during the course of the evening. After that, he started giving them away.

One of the best things about cycle for Willie was the chance to learn from the best. One of his trainers was a man who had learnt from the Vietnam SAS vets.

When I first met Sam it was unreal. He showed us things – not from a book but in a practical way that was simple and hit home: why we did this formation, why we came up in this way, why when crap hits the fan we break out into a certain area and stuff like that. You couldn't just look at these things on the blackboard and understand them. He physically took us out on the ground and showed us. And he explained it all in a way that we could understand.

He got me to draw an eyeball.

'Who remembers from their med course what the eyeball looks like?'

I got up there and I drew an eyeball and it looked like a tadpole or a sperm on its way to fertilise the egg. We all got a laugh out of that. But then he showed us on the eye how it works and explained why we see things, what catches our eye, what we see in low light and how long it takes your eye to adjust when you go from bright light to complete darkness. It might take seven to eight minutes for your eyes to start slowly adjusting, but at the end of 40 minutes you're totally adjusted to the light that you're travelling with. The point being that your eye needs time to adjust, and when you go into something where the light is different, you should try to take that time.

They always say if a bright light comes, you should close one eye, so at least you've got an eye that's already adjusted, and you'll have a balance while the other one's starting to tune back in. That's the same with your night vision goggles, because they are using all the ambient light, from the stars and the moon and any other source they can find, for you to be able to see. If it's pitch black, you can still see with NVGs, but if there's a bit of starlight and some moon it's almost like daylight, and when you take them off it's dark, because your eyes have been subjected to light. It's the small things like that that make your job a bit easier, because you understand the principles.

Sam had a high opinion of Willie from this stage, too. The younger man would do everything and anything. If there was cleaning up to be done, Willie would be cleaning up, before reporting back to say, 'It's done.' If there was anything else to be taken care of, he would do that too. He would work all day long without being asked. His performance, attitude and skills were up to the standard required. There is no top student on cycle. That is not the SAS way – all contribute to the outcomes.

Alongside CQB, resistance to interrogation (RTI) is the part of cycle that attracts most outside curiosity. After being pursued across the countryside and going through any number of stressful situations, the trainees are captured and interrogated. Both mental and physical means are used. If SAS members are notoriously men of few words when talking about their work and training, that is garrulous by comparison to how they clam up on the subject of RTI.

It's not the real thing. It may even be completely different from any kind of real thing a badged member would experience if captured. But to those who have been through it, it's better than having no experience at all, however pale a facsimile. The real thing may be more violent, but the RTI training gives them something to guide them through and some ideas on how to act. It also lets them learn a little about themselves and how they might handle interrogation. And everyone has to go through it to become a member of the SAS. Although Willie didn't like it, he got through it okay.

That day, a few hours after his RTI, Willie began his first leave. A few hours later, he and a couple of mates were at Ericsson Stadium watching the Warriors play the Rabbitohs.

'This is surreal,' he thought.

CHAPTER ELEVEN

INITIATE

Willie was badged on 20 September 2002, in the presence of his close family, at a ceremony held in one of the Rennie Lines hangars. It was a big event that year. As well as those getting badged, several Group members were to receive medals and recognition – of the kind that are not listed in the honours lists that appear in newspapers.

Given what it represents, and what a man has had to accomplish for this moment to occur, the transition to badged member is a remarkably simple ritual. The soldier takes off one beret and receives another, along with the blue belt which only he and his peers are entitled to wear. The badge in question is that common to all SAS troops around the world – the flaming sword, above the motto 'Who Dares Wins'.

In the presence of the Chief of the Army – now head of the New Zealand Defence Force – Lieutenant General Jerry Mateparae, himself a former badged member, the Colonel Commandant of the unit presented Willie his beret and badge.

For those who receive the honour, it is invariably the proudest moment of their lives. They look around at the others who have come through with them. They have spent a lot of time together, under the most trying of circumstances, performing the most challenging of deeds. This is why the bond between them is so strong. Yet it is equally as strong with the others in the hangar, who have been wearing this beret and belt for many years, for they too went through the same process to reach this point.

The newly badged know there is no time to relax. Unless they keep working as hard as they already have been, and continue to improve themselves at every stage of their career, the SAS will not want to know them. On this day, however, it is hard to think of any achievement to match what is taking place, let alone surpass it, although Willie would ultimately find one.

The SAS has most definitely changed over the years. Not only has it become more discreet, but it has also become less identified with the intimidating, steely-eyed behaviour of past generations of members. It acknowledges that those in the unit may have partners and children; that they may endure psychological effects from their experiences which need to be taken into account; that provision may need to be made for their lives after service. There are even comfort stops during regimental dinners these days.

By its very silence, the SAS allowed rumours about its nature to flourish. It would rather there were no rumours, but to deal with them head on is to open a conversation it would prefer not to have.

Instead, it has allowed a little more light to be shed on its activities through some tightly controlled media exposure. Now those who spread the rumours know they are just that. The organisation itself has nothing to hide that doesn't need to be hidden.

There is a comparison to be made with, for example, an elite sports team. If it had an open training session every day, come Saturday everybody would know their moves. And they would lose. The SAS doesn't lose. For them, losing is not about going to the changing rooms and having a beer and saying we missed out – losing is about bringing somebody home in a bag. It simply isn't an option. And some things about their operation – their capabilities, techniques and tactics, and the way they operate – they do keep closely to themselves.

In Willie's case, family and some friends knew he was in the SAS. Members use discretion about what they reveal and to whom. But he had other friends who did not even know he was in the Army until it had been announced that he had won the Victoria Cross.

Despite recent changes and ongoing evolution, many of the guiding principles established by David Stirling are still a crucial part of the Group's ethos.

One of the most important elements is egalitarianism. This attribute would have been more marked with the original SAS, whose members came from a more strictly class-defined society, but even in a country like New Zealand it is unusual for a branch of the Army to take such little note of rank or station.

Similarly, competitiveness between members is a constant. They will compete over anything – whether it's how fast you can pull the pistol out or who can get the tightest grouping on a target. When the men are running or doing PT, they are always competing, because that's how they go that extra distance. It keeps them alive and stops things from getting mundane.

And whoever wins in these competitions, they are not allowed to get ideas above themselves. Humility is another key SAS virtue and it is emphasised for new Group members, who are as likely to start their career sweeping a floor as they are parachuting into unknown terrain.

You have to start at the bottom. You push the broom when you're the new fella on the block, and you make sure the shed is clean at the end of every day. Even though I've been here for a long time now, I still sweep floors and so do the others. It's something we always do for the lads.

You are proud about everything you do, including sweeping. You've just been given your beret and your belt and it's your first day in the shed. This is just another thing you have learned through cycle. As soon as the work is over, it's time to tidy up. You won't go anywhere until everything is clean and tidy.

You could become complacent and not stay switched on, but that's the quickest way to get thrown out of here. We handle a lot of weapons. The work we do is dangerous, but we are trained at it and we know all the safety precautions that have to be carried out to be able to perform it. If you get complacent about it, then you're going to get hurt or hurt someone else, so that doesn't happen.

Everyone makes mistakes but we learn from them. Integrity is the biggest thing we have. When you get busted, you face the music. You step up and say, 'I did it.' And you accept your punishment. Don't expect anyone else to be punished because you didn't step up to the mark. Don't let someone else be your fall guy. That's gutless. I learnt that from the boys I hung around with growing up. And I learnt it from my father and from old Reuben, too. You didn't bluff them because they could see right through you straight away.

We don't have any room for someone who thinks they're the man – because we've all been through the same training, and we all share the same environment. When we see young fellas coming in now, off selection or cycle, they might not know who we are, but we know what they've been through, and they know when they look at us that we've done exactly the same as them.

If you're wearing the beret, you're an equal – that's how the boys treat each other. Just wearing the uniform makes you part of this family. Half the men here I didn't know before I was badged, but we all know that when one of our guys needs support we'll be there. He just has to have the same colour uniform.

It's not like civilian life. If your mate can't depend on you in the military, people can lose lives. The only thing you can lose in the outside world is money. And you can always earn that back. It's pretty hard to bring someone back from the dead, though.

Yet we're each other's biggest critics, and we criticise each other to make each other better. There's nothing like your mate saying, 'Hey, bro, that's rubbish.' You'll ask him what he means and he'll explain, but it's up to you whether you take any notice of that or not.

The reason this place is always exciting for me is that I'm learning some-thing new every day. Your sergeants and staff sergeants above you manage your career to make sure you're not becoming stagnant in a position. They keep you moving up. Everybody has their strengths and their weaknesses and we complement each other. People go where they can be the most use. Everybody doesn't have to be good at everything. But everyone tries to be.

They teach us to think outside the square in the SAS. To me, instructions are a good guideline, but *only* a guideline. They're not something you always have to stick to.

There is a maverick streak that's a big part of the tradition. I learnt a bit about that from watching some of the outlaw types I've known in my life. So I think: 'What sort of people do they want in the defence force? Do they want someone who can't cross the line? Or do they want somebody who they know will cross a line if that is what needs to happen? If he sticks to the rules all the way, then will he be able to accomplish his mission?'

I think that you need to be realistic to be able to achieve those ends, because combat is sometimes not a pretty sight. We are taught and know that good training and sound decisions based on what is morally and ethically correct will always carry the day.

CHAPTER TWELVE

BADGED MEMBER

Willie was badged on a Friday, told he was going to Afghanistan the following Monday, and on his way there within a week. He wasn't meant to go, but the badging ceremony proved too much for one Group member who was. Drills and parades are not a big part of SAS tradition, and having to stand still for hours does not come naturally to men whose default setting is action. Willie heard, but did not see, when a Group member who was supposed to go to Afghanistan lost consciousness. The only sound he made was a faint gasp as he lost consciousness, fell backwards and cracked his skull.

No one moved, neither front or back of him nor on either side. Eventually, squadron members picked him up and got him to hospital, where he was diagnosed with a fractured skull.

Willie assumed the worst when he was summoned to see the Officer Commanding and Squadron Sergeant Major the next Monday. He tried to think what he could have done over the weekend that might have got him into trouble. The OC and SSM were waiting for him.

'Did you learn anything on cycle?' asked the OC.

'Yeah, I learnt heaps, sir.'

'How would you like to go to Afghanistan?'

Willie was speechless but his expression made his answer plain.

'What about your family? Do you think they'd mind if you go?'

'I'm going,' said Willie.

He couldn't believe his luck. To be going on an operation so soon was beyond his highest expectations. The dreams that had carried him through the rigours and privations of the previous months were coming true. Afghanistan, wherever – he would have gone to the moon in bare feet if he'd been asked to. This was what it was all about.

The New Zealand public knew very little about the details of the SAS's Afghan deployment as part of the US-led Operation Enduring Freedom. They were to learn a lot more later when Willie Apiata was awarded the Victoria Cross, unavoidably dragging it into the spotlight.

But his family knew where he was, and while they were happy for him, they spent a worried few months. Compared to the ease and regularity of communications when he was in East Timor with the Territorials, contact with family was restricted. While the men were allowed to communicate with whoever they wanted, facilities for doing so were limited. Also, they were busy.

Mail came by plane, which was not that often. When it did come, Willie could usually expect to find his consignment of lamb's tongues and corned beef. In the absence of definite information, it was easy for fears and suspicions to fester back home. Also, his partner knew that if she did hear anything officially, it would most probably be bad news.

Just as there had been for Willie's tour of East Timor, there was a short period of pre-deployment training plus acclimatisation and rehearsing in country on arrival.

However, getting to his destination, on a New Zealand Air Force Hercules, wasn't nearly as straightforward as getting on the mission.

From time to time, the US Navy Support Facility at Diego Garcia sees a New Zealand plane stopping to refuel on its week-long journey to Afghanistan. The lumbering, noisy – those being transported wear earplugs – Hercules have two crews who are only permitted to fly a certain number of hours. Even with rotation they must occasionally stop overnight.

Diego Garcia is a picture-book tropical island in the Indian Ocean that has become an important military refuelling point. Willie was seriously impressed by the show of force on the island, which appeared to him covered by bombers and fighter jets, with huge B-52s flying overhead. Surely, these people ruled the skies.

The group also stopped in the Middle East where Willie was drawn into the market streets and fascinated by the locals, particularly women in full burkhas, who nevertheless managed to glower intimidatingly if he so much as glanced at them in a way they deemed inappropriate.

But for Willie, the ever-eager student, seeking from those more experienced than himself the sort of knowledge that can't be found in books, the best part of the first tour was being amongst so many soldiers with so much experience. The feeling was mutual. There is no point in being a teacher if you haven't got a student, and for the elders of the SAS, imbued with the tradition of handing on the knowledge they have striven to acquire, Willie was the perfect pupil. His might not have been the first name on the list of those it would be good to have in Afghanistan, but he was obviously near the top.

Sam was already there with the first part of the New Zealand contingent. He observed that the newly badged member hit the ground running, willing to do anything and everything around the compound. If no instruction was forthcoming, he would go and find something to do. Eventually, Sam explained that operations was not training. Willie needed to slow down and relax so he'd be ready for the real thing.

Willie was so eager partly because of the presence of such a high number of senior badged members. He was working side by side with men who had trained him, and he wanted to prove their faith in him had not been misplaced. The point was also made that, although it might be natural to feel you are not a bona fide SAS member until you have been in an operation, the senior men do not see it that way. As far as they are concerned – when you're in, you're in. After all, in the early 90s there were men who had been in the SAS for 20 years and had never gone on an operation, simply because there was no operation to go on. That is not the case nowadays.

Another guy's bad luck resulted in me getting a seat on that plane. There were just two of us who went from my cycle, the officer and myself. I went with the elders. I was the greenest one on the block.

The first thing I remember is that when we landed in the country one of the old fellas here said: 'You've finished cycle. There's no more "Staff" and that here. You call us by our first names.' And that was really hard to get used to because I had just spent nine months calling these guys 'Staff'. I had respected them and that's why I called them that, regardless of whether they were just a corporal. It felt funny to now be calling them by their first names. But after a few days you get into the groove. I got to know them a hell of a lot better. And I understand we call each other by our first names because we're all mates, regardless of rank.

My attitude to work was to do whatever needed to be done, and then a little bit more. I got to use my backyard mechanic's skills a lot. It was a bit like Radar from *Mash* – you try to have things done before anyone asks you to do them. And it's competitive. You're trying to beat the other guy to get things done and you're annoyed if you think of something and the other bugger's already gone and done it.

You don't mind how much you do, because the whole experience is pure adrenalin. You're hanging on every word that your senior guys are saying about how things are done. After that tour, a lot of those old fellas' time with the SAS was up, and they moved on. So it was really special to be able to be on the ground with them. They enveloped me in their way of life and culture. It meant I could still learn heaps.

When we flew into our first patrol, we were airlifted in and drove out of the plane in our vehicles. Before we landed, the pilot came up to Sam and said, 'I have to apologise – we're going to be seven seconds late.'

We stayed there for about a month, then they flew in again, and we drove back on the planes and took off. The aircraft was only on the ground for two or three minutes. When we were waiting for it, it was blacked out, so we couldn't see it coming. But we could hear it, and then suddenly, through all this dust, it appeared.

The countryside is beautiful. If you didn't live in it, it could be the most fearsome experience of your life, but for those people it's easy. You see them in the desert carrying their four-litre water containers. Where are they going? And how far have they come? They don't have maps. They know where they're going, and where to find water.

It didn't take long to realise how vast Afghanistan is. The desert isn't flat. You can get up on vantage points and see that it stretches away forever. They had to be tough people to survive there. It's no wonder they've produced warriors who have never been conquered, even though so many people have tried. They also know the shortcuts, and they know their way around the caves in the mountains. There must be caves cut through all that terrain. It reminds me of some of the old trails in New Zealand that the Maori used to use.

The Afghans are great riders, but you didn't see many horses unless the people were wealthy. Mostly it was camels for transport and just about anything else. We were mucking around once trying to catch a baby camel. It made a hell of a noise, and its mother must have heard and come over. Suddenly she was spitting big hunks of green sticky snot at us.

The Bedouins travel around, put up their tents, graze their stock and then move on. They have their livestock with them – goats, sheep and dogs – and they bring them all in around their tents at night. Then the dogs become guard dogs. The sheep and goats know where to go so they'll be safe when it gets dark. Everyone is doing what has been done for hundreds of years.

Another thing I really liked there was their dogs. They were like a cross between a hyena and a donkey – the hyena for looks and donkey for size. They are used to protect livestock, and are absolutely ferocious. They love chasing motorbikes, which gets dangerous if you're riding at night because you might see them coming but there is no guarantee you will.

You can see a lot of change when you go from the highlands, where we patrolled, down to the lowlands, where the cities are. The lower you go, the more Westernised things get. Up the top, the people will dig up the earth with a bullock pulling a shaped branch. A bit further down, you'll see a bullock pulling a plough. And further down again, you'll see someone using a tractor to plough the fields. But in many parts, where there are roadworks, the road-working machinery will be just a man and a donkey.

We tried to go around with an open mind about the people and what we would find. Partly it's an adventure, but it could also be dangerous. Our job was to patrol, meeting locals and gathering information that might be useful in the hunt for the Taliban. It wasn't all cruising around seeing the sights and playing with camels though. There are land mines around. We hit one once. We lost a vehicle, and one of the blokes lost his leg.

On a patrol, you have Dumvees – special ops vehicles that are basically Humvees with a D for desert – and there are three or four blokes in each one. We have our own vehicles now but in 2004 we had vehicles borrowed from the US. My first truck was called *Taiaha*, the next one *Taniwha*. We give them names because those are our call signs when we are out. Then there are the outriders, scouts on motorbikes who go ahead to check things out. Everyone gets to do everything, which I really like. I've been a driver and a gunner. The only thing I haven't been yet is a vehicle commander.

We always had a tight schedule to keep to, and it wasn't unusual to be on the go constantly for 36 hours if we had to get somewhere. Once, it took us that long to get out of a single valley. That was another example of something you did in selection being exactly what you do on an operation – in this case, keeping going for long periods without sleep. And with water short and us being so far out, sometimes it would be weeks before we could have any kind of wash.

At one stage we were so far away from anything that the helicopters which were flying out to resupply us had to refuel in mid-air on the way. The fuel planes would fly out to meet them. Then the helicopters would drop our stuff off, turn around and have another mid-air refuel on the way back again. That's the sort of equipment the Americans have at their disposal and the kind of thing they do. For our country, the SAS is regarded as pretty well resourced, but if we had half their equipment we'd be able to do some amazing things.

We did make ourselves a battle truck while we were there. The idea was to use it as a mother craft for the patrols to work from, like a supply wagon with extra fuel and ammo. We put a turret on it and made mounts for our GPMG (general purpose machine gun). It was built out of stuff we scavenged from the dump where the Americans threw out what they didn't want. They'd thrown out old bunk beds made from tubular steel – just what we needed. We cut them up and turned them into mounts.

When they saw what we'd done, they wanted to know where we got our parts from. We told them it was from what they had thrown out, but they didn't believe us. They were good dudes and I liked them a lot. They all smoked big Cuban cigars.

One of the things about the SAS is the idea that you keep things simple – travel light and in small groups so you can adapt easily when things change; get in and out of places quickly. Modern technology has made that worse, not better. Our packs are so heavy now, because of what everyone has to carry. In the old days, sigs had the heaviest load, because they had to carry radios. After that it was the medics with all their gear. Now everyone is weighed down with all sorts of bits and pieces.

Some of our patrols were at high altitudes, and at 15,000 feet the air is really thin. Being a smoker was an advantage for once, because for some reason having a cigarette makes it easier to breathe at that height. I never saw rain there, but I saw snow and sandstorms. One night, we put up a shelter because we were expecting it to rain. I got up first because I was on sentry and walked out, and everything was covered in snow. That was good, because you could make snowballs and stock them up to hassle the outriders with when they rode past your truck.

Sandstorms are weird. Once we saw one coming when we weren't too far from the compound, so we raced back ahead of it. We got back and suddenly it was there. It passed right over us and then it was gone again, as though it had never happened.

I bought quite a few shemaghs – the pieces of cloth Afghans use for head-gear – back home with me. They're a novelty here, but are essential over there. They keep the sand out of your face and protect you from the sun, which can be fierce. Those guys don't have chapstick, and your lips would soon be cracked and your eyes burnt if you didn't protect them with something. That's also why they grow their beards – it's protection for your face.

After our last job in Kabul, we stopped in the Middle East for three days. Before we go home to our families they try to give us a couple of days off somewhere, so we can relax, talk about things together and be ready to re-engage with our loved ones. It works, otherwise you come home with a lot of energy that you should have left behind.

We landed in Whenuapai without any fanfare as we normally do and went back to the compound to get our gear squared away. Once we were good to go again we were then released for some leave. You've done your work, the job's finished and your next focus is going home. You're glad to see your partner but you've been away a long time. Everyone has their own routine: I had mine, she had hers, and then you have to fit in with each other. It's like starting all over again. Every time you get back, for the first couple of weeks, you're waited on hand and foot. Then one morning, bang, it's like you've never been away.

Back home, months of worry had dragged by for Willie's family. Sometimes it was bad, other times it was not so bad. Separations like this are always easier on the one who is away. Although you miss your family, there is a plethora of new experiences to take your mind off it. You are the one doing the novel, diverting things. They are the ones doing what they've always done. Separation is easier when you have interesting work to stay focused on.

It's only in the down times that you stop to think about those who are so far away. Even if he had been able to call home daily, Willie is not much of a phone person. Ten minutes on the line counts as a marathon. If he has something to tell or ask someone, he would rather do it face to face, and he has even been known to drive from Auckland to Wellington to do it.

There was one further thing back home to occupy Willie's mind while he was away. Not long before he left, his partner told him she was pregnant. He was well aware that had made things even lonelier for her and that she'd had a lot to cope with that would have been easier if he had been there to support her. But SAS member is not the only job that keeps couples apart for long periods when they would rather be together. Not long after Willie's return, with the arrival of their baby not far away, his partner moved from Whakatane to Auckland to be near him.

Their son was born on 20 April 2003. The boy was named after Willie's partner's father and grandfather, and Willie's grandfather.

Willie was entitled to 10 days' leave to get to know his son, but afterward was thrown straight back into the vortex of SAS duties. First he was off for six weeks at Trentham, a student doing his junior NCO course – he came top of leadership in the first and second parts of that – then briefly home again before being sent on a tracking course.

He knew he was getting the easy end of the parenting deal. His partner coped with all the trials of a baby's first months, and by the time Willie was home for a substantial period his son was a happy baby who was already sleeping through the night.

Willie's second tour in Afghanistan occupied several months in early 2004. His son turned one on April 20, and although Willie could not be there for his son's birthday the family made a video and sent it to him. He relished being able to see, if only from a distance, his boy's first birthday party. There was no express service. The video, like other mail, arrived with the next plane bringing supplies. It might have been a month and a half after the event, but it was better than nothing.

It was just another in the list of landmarks in his boy's early life – crawling, first steps – that Willie missed out on because he was doing his duty. On his return from the second tour, the two would have to get to know each other all over again. He missed his son tremendously, especially given the amount a child grows and changes in the second half of its first year. Willie came home as a stranger to his son and it took days for the young boy to get used to him.

There had been more phones and computer terminals available in Afghanistan this time, and Willie managed to communicate with his partner more regularly. But it was a mixed blessing. If there were things going wrong, there was nothing he could do, but at least there was always the appointed contact on the scene – someone arranged by the Army, before a soldier is deployed, to keep an eye on things at home for him and help his partner if required.

The only thing that would see a soldier brought home early was death or serious injury in the family. It was hard, but at least the rules were clear and everyone knew where they stood. You might not like it, but you didn't complain. Especially not Willie – because this time he was lucky to come home at all.

CHAPTER THIRTEEN

GOOD SOLDIER

Because it earned Willie Apiata the first Victoria Cross for New Zealand, what happened to his troop in a portion of Afghan desert early one morning in 2004 has become the most publicised case of contact with an enemy in New Zealand SAS history. Yet much is still not known about it, such as exactly where and when it happened. That is why Willie's medal bears on its obverse not the date of the action for which it was awarded, as is customary, but the date on which it was announced: 2 July 2007.

It is possible to describe the feat that drew the accolade very simply: Willie picked up a mortally wounded comrade and carried him uphill for 70 metres under heavy fire to medical aid. He then re-armed himself and returned to the conflict. Willie himself is capable of telling those who ask that what happened is 'all in the citation'. There was, of course, much more to it than that.

The action occurred on what had been a day like any other on the troop's tour. They had been on patrol for a couple of weeks and had visited a village where they spoke to the residents and asked if they could set up a meeting with the local commanders and other head people. They were there to gather information, and this was customary practice. Although they carried guns and ammunition, their most important weapon on this mission was their radio, and their primary objective was to pass on the data they gathered. They were not rampaging through the Afghan countryside shooting at rocks in case they were Taliban. As they saw it, they were there to help.

Local elections were not far off, making them a natural topic for ice-breaking conversation. As one who was there describes it, the villagers' way of doing things was 'very Polynesian': lots of chatting and cups of tea, building rapport with small talk, before getting down to the real business. They agreed to meet again the next day.

However, there had been a suggestion that those in the village were sympathetic to the Taliban. The men who were involved in the action will never know for sure whether they had been identified as targets while they were there. However, they had only taken a small number of vehicles along, and anyone seeing them could easily have been misled into thinking the troop was much smaller than it was.

There was nothing covert about this action. If the troop had wanted to remain hidden, they would have done things very differently. They could have confined themselves to using night vision gear, moving only after dark and resting during the day, camouflaged from sight. But they had already been to the village, made themselves known and made it clear they weren't trying to hide anything.

With no reason to think extra precautions needed to be taken, as a lay-up position for the night they chose a location that, although it was defensible, was not concealed. It was a barren spot, with not a tree in sight, but the undulating terrain meant there were areas they could not see into. The aim was to find some high ground. The troop identified some features that gave them all-round protection, but that also meant there were places where someone could get through. There is seldom a perfect place to lay up. For anyone watching them with hostile intent, the location would have added to the impression the troop was smaller than it actually was. It is also possible the troop misjudged the territory. One theory is that they had strayed across an invisible ethnic border into a region whose inhabitants were more hostile than those they had encountered earlier.

Before settling down for the night, there was work to be done. The troop staff sergeant went over the day's events with the commanders, discussing what had happened, why, and what they needed to do about it. Every point in the action raises numerous contingencies that have to be accounted for, and the next day's activities have to be planned. A detailed brief of 'actions on' is always prepared and these are gone over before patrols move on again. On this occasion, the next day's activities would be straightforward – the troop would return to the village to meet with the elders as arranged. A sentry roster was prepared to outline who would do what overnight.

There's also a daily accounting of food, water and fuel consumption, based on which the troop knows what it can count on being able to do in the next few days, and what it might need to arrange to have flown in. Patrols such as this do not commute back and forth from a central base but stay out for long periods. They cannot take enough supplies with them, so have to be resupplied en route by helicopter.

In the event of contact, a US special forces air guy with the troop

– attached because, for this purpose, it is easier for Americans to talk to Americans, especially in cases involving complex US assets – will be responsible for communications with close air support or anything else that may be necessary to close things down. Any of us know how to do it but these guys are the experts.

All had gone well and the night had been as uneventful as those preceding it. The staff sergeant rose for his turn at sentry a couple of hours before daybreak. Suddenly, the sky exploded in a barrage of fire from rocket-propelled grenades (RPGs) – so much that it was impossible to guess how many were being fired or, at first, where they were coming from. They went over the troop's heads but there was also small arms fire, identifiable from its distinctive whizzing sound, coming between the vehicles.

The first priority when something like this happens is not to retaliate – which is one's automatic reaction – but to work out as far as possible exactly what is going on in order to make the most effective response. Most importantly, communications have to be established in order to arrange air support.

A number of the vehicles departed, which was the drill. That left the staff sergeant and forward air controller trying to obtain air cover. Everything around may be frantic and chaotic, but it's not something that can be done in a couple of moments. Minutes will go by before any sort of order can be brought to the scene.

In the first few moments, Willie's vehicle, with its three occupants, had taken a direct hit from an RPG and was on fire. The insurgents didn't have high-tech NVG, and they didn't need it. Willie's wagon was a blazing torch lighting up the scene. It quickly became a lead magnet.

My wagon was called the *Almighty*. The others slept on the ground, but I always slept on the bonnet with all my gear, because it was nice and flat and warm. The first thing I knew about it was when the wagon was hit – I got blasted out of my sleeping bag, and found myself standing up with the bag around my ankles. My gear had been scattered with the force of the blast.

I don't know how long those buggers had been there waiting. Only they know that. All I know is we got woken up really early. The first thing I thought was: 'Where's all this stuff coming from?' I could see that they were just in front of us, but there was other stuff coming from further away as well. And for some reason, our wagon was getting hit from that side.

Identifying where the buggers are coming from and how far away they are when you're reacting to enemy fire is part of our preparation. The training gives you the tools, and what you do depends on what tools you have in your toolbox at the time. They can give you all the training in the world, but it's just a guide to help you get out of this sort of situation. It's up to the individual what he does in the moment. You can make a difference, or you can make it worse. It's combat. All the training you get is for that eventual day when the crap may hit the fan, and you know if you're there that it's not going to be nice.

We were briefed up every night about what to do if we got hit from this direction or that direction. If all else fails you have a Plan B and just crash out. But you always have something set out. So I knew what to do, but I won't say I was cool, calm and collected.

This fire was coming down all around, and I did what I thought was best. Two of us had made it to the back of the wagon. The first thing you want to do is account for your men. Are we all okay? I had just said, 'Where's our man?' when my other mate came flopping around the corner. I could see he was seriously injured. I could hear it. You could turn a tap on right now and hear the water hitting the sink – that was the sound of his blood pouring out and hitting the ground.

I don't know what tore through his arm, but it was a massive wound. It had hit an artery. And if you hit one of those, it's going to empty your body because it's an open outlet. The blood can no longer circulate. It's going to keep coming up until there's nothing left. We needed to be able to block it.

I said to my mate, 'Go and grab us a first field dressing off the wagon,' because we had them taped all over it.

He moved forward and grabbed his webbing. But because our wagon was on fire, when he did that, they saw his shadow and suddenly the small arms and the gunfire coming towards us intensified tenfold. You could feel every round ripping through the vehicle. I'm amazed he made it.

I knew we had to move. With the wagon being on fire it could only protect us for so long. There were that many RPG rounds rocking it, hitting it one after the other. With the flames, we were about the only thing those guys could see. They could see the flash off other weapons, and they could probably see the fire from our other vehicles, but the thing that made the best target was the thing that was in flames.

We were still at the back of the wagon, but sooner or later one of us was going to take a round if we stayed there. When our wagon got hit, one dude tried to get up to his gun to start returning fire, and I pulled him back. I said, 'No way, bro.' He would have made a perfect target.

Our boys couldn't fully suppress these guys until we got out of the way, because we were right in front – directly in their line of fire. I knew if we stayed any longer, we were going to be in really deep trouble. Another vehicle had come up into a position where he could fire. When I heard his GPMG going hard, one long continuous burst, that's when I knew we had our opportunity. So I said, 'We're out of here – we gotta go!' My mate agreed.

When we started, I had my injured mate's arm over my shoulder, but he was in so much shock and had lost so much blood, he couldn't walk. He went only about five or 10 paces, perhaps not even that. And then he collapsed. We were out in the open at this stage, with firing going on all around us, so I picked him up and put him on my shoulder.

ABOVE: The CDF, the Boss and I face the press.

BELOW: The Boss and I have a chat with the Minister.

ABOVE: Dignitaries at the Investiture.

BELOW: The Colonel Commandant, me, Minister, Boss and RSM front and centre.

ABOVE: The inscription on the back of my Victoria Cross.

FAR LEFT: The medal as presented to me before it was mounted.

LEFT: The statuette.

BELOW: Victoria Cross at home at Rennie Lines next to the carving and the trophy room.

ABOVE: Te Whanau Apanui hand me over to the Nga Puhi at Waitangi.

RIGHT: Treaty Grounds.

BELOW: En route to the Treaty Grounds.

ABOVE: Palmerston North Boys High School perform a haka for our arrival.

BELOW: Conducting a medals' parade for my nieces and nephews on New Years Eve 2007.

ABOVE: Getting acquainted with Lord Michael Ashcroft, KCMG.

BELOW: Laying a wreath on Lord Freyberg's grave – what an honour.

ABOVE: Back to work – training in confined spaces.

BELOW: Dive training with Amphibious Troop.

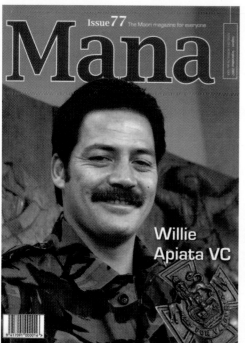

Issue **77** The Maori magazine for everyone

Mana

Willie
Apiata VC

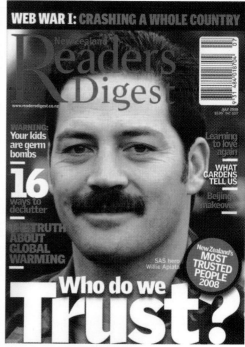

WEB WAR I: CRASHING A WHOLE COUNTRY

New Zealand's

Readers
Digest

www.readersdigest.co.nz

JULY 2008
$5.95* INC GST

WARNING:
Your kids
are germ
bombs

16
ways to
declutter

THE TRUTH
ABOUT
GLOBAL
WARMING

Learning
to love
again

**WHAT
GARDENS
TELL US**

Beijing
makeover

SAS hero
Willie Apiata

New Zealand's
**MOST
TRUSTED
PEOPLE
2008**

Who do we
Trust?

RELUCTANT
HERO

CPL.
WILLIE
APIATA, VC

THE EXCLUSIVE
STORY BEHIND
NZ'S NEWEST
HERO. NARRATED
BY TEMUERA
MORRISON.

DVD

In the Army, they teach you to stay low to get out of the way of bullets, but this time we needed to move quickly, because I didn't know how fast these dudes were coming up the hill to attack us, or how many of them there were. I did know they were very close though. So the quicker we got out of the line of fire, the quicker the boys could concentrate on them. And we needed to get to safety, or at least to first aid, as quickly as we could.

All three of us moved up the hill. You can recognise the different wagons, even at night, because you've been working with them for so long. And as we hit the crest of the hill, I could see the one with the advanced med guy. So I went straight there and called the med's name. When he answered, I said, 'Look after our mate.' Their wagon had been laid up in a position where it wasn't quite in the firefight, so he was in a position to start treating him.

The commander of the vehicle I left my mate at had gone to assist another one of the boys who'd been injured and was being brought back to the rear for medical attention as well. I saw his GPMG still hanging on the side of the wagon, so I grabbed it and a big link of ammunition and went straight back to where the boys were firing on the other side of the hill, suppressing these guys, and got into it.

At the time, it makes you angry, and anger makes you move forward. If you're that brassed off, there's no way you're going to take a step back. The one thing you want to do is keep going. I think anger helps you a lot in a case like that, where you see your mate hurt. When I'd finally dropped him off, and I went and re-armed myself, I was just angry that they had done that to us. I was thinking: 'They hurt my mate and woke us up early in the morning', and I wanted to get back and give them a seeing-to.

The other guy who was with me felt the same. As soon as we hit the rise, when he knew my injured mate and I were fine, he peeled off to another wagon, asked one of the boys for a weapon and got back into the fight. I'd say he was angry too.

There was just a scratch on me. Nothing hit me. I can't explain why I didn't get hit. None of us did, when we were crossing that hill through the fire. My mate didn't get hit when he was on my back and the other guy didn't get hit. It's a miracle we made it. Everyone could see us coming in the light from the burning vehicle. All the weapons firing lit up the area even more.

Those guys bit off more than they could chew. They thought we were half the size we were, because they couldn't see the other vehicles. They had thought: 'There's only a few of them – let's go and smash them.' They didn't know who they were hitting. And they were sent packing, with their tails between their legs. We were still firing long after they'd stopped.

A lot of guys in the Army have done lots of peace trips and never seen combat. Some guys have been in ambushes and have come into contact with militias, but not very many. Afterwards, you try to leave it all in the country. What he does is the measure of a man, but how he deals with it later is a measure of the man, too. We all deal with things differently, and it's each to his own. You can't tell a guy how to react. It's going to be your own personal experience when it does go down.

As day broke, the troop was getting itself back together. When the air support finally arrived it turned out to be an unwieldy B-1 bomber, which was not ideal for tracking down whoever was now bouncing over the dunes in a Hilux, away from where the attack had taken place. But everyone knew how lucky they had been to have sustained no fatalities. Half a dozen men could have been killed in a heartbeat.

A perimeter patrol showed there had been some enemy killed in action, which meant due process had to be gone through. Evidence is gathered to record the scene and clarify to superiors what has taken place. Lost and damaged equipment is noted. Within a short time, a Chinook brought out another vehicle to replace the *Almighty* and the patrol was back on the road by 5 p.m.

My injured mate was taken straight to Germany, went to hospital and they brought him home from there. He was fine. You're not left wondering. You get to hear what's happened: 'The boys are doing well, they're recovering.'

We didn't have much time to stop and think. We were trying to reconstitute ourselves. We'd lost two wagons, so we had another one brought in, got it all kitted out on the ground, and then we were off again.

It's a long time to get to the end of something like that, because there are a lot of phases to go through. The end is when you finally drive out, and your wheels roll back into the camp. The patrol doesn't finish until you're back in the base and you unload your weapons.

There wasn't a lot of time to think about what had happened. It was a life-changing experience, but I didn't think about it too much until I got home. You still want to focus on the job while you're there. But after something like that, you're different, because you've already been stung once.

On that day everything that I've learnt in my life – from all the old people around me, the old chap and my old man, and through all the guys that have trained me in the Army, through cycle and afterward – it all came down to that one small piece of ground and that little portion of time. Then you knew that everything was drawn into yourself to enable you to accomplish those things. All those other people were there beside you to help you, to teach you that small bit of something that helped you cover that ground, carry that guy and get him out of there in that one moment.

After the contact, we did a few more patrols. We didn't come home early or late. We came home when we had done our job. And when I walked off the plane, my mate was the first dude I saw. He was there waiting with his wife. It's so painful when they give you a big hug and say, 'Thank you for carrying my husband to safety.' They got married when he came home. It was the best thing in the world to see him standing on the tarmac. We went and had a few beers. I would see him every day after that at work, and every day was a blessing.

They have psychologists and psychiatrists and different people you can talk to. We have to – that's the process – but I don't like it. They are people of the mind who are trying to get in there, to see if you're unstable, or the next level up, some sort of psycho. We all deal with things in our own way. I know any day now could be my last breath, and knowing that makes me really appreciate my whanau.

One other thing happened after the contact. My Troop Commander who was there at the contact said he was going to put me up for a medal.

'No thanks,' I said.

'It's not going to be a Victoria Cross or anything,' he said. 'But you deserve a medal.'

'I don't care about a medal. I'm just glad our bro's okay and we got out alive.'

'You're being put forward, Willie, regardless.'

'That's your decision, sir.'

SPECIAL HONOURS LIST – 2 JULY 2007

NEW ZEALAND GALLANTRY AWARDS

The Queen has been pleased to approve the following

New Zealand Gallantry Awards:

VICTORIA CROSS FOR NEW ZEALAND (V.C.)

Corporal Bill Henry APIATA (M181550)

1st New Zealand Special Air Service Group

Rennie Lines

Private Bag 25

PAPAKURA

Citation

Lance Corporal (now Corporal) Apiata was, in 2004, part of a New Zealand Special Air Service (NZSAS) Troop on patrol in Afghanistan, which laid up in defensive formation for the night. At approximately 0315 hours, the Troop was attacked by a group of about twenty enemy fighters, who had approached by stealth using the cover of undulating ground in pitch darkness. Rocket-propelled grenades struck two of the Troop's vehicles, destroying one and immobilising the other. The opening strike was followed by dense and persistent machine gun and automatic rifle fire from close range. The attack then continued using further rocket-propelled grenades and machine gun and rifle fire. The initial attack was directed at the vehicle where Lance Corporal Apiata was stationed. He was blown off the bonnet by the impact of rocket propelled grenades striking the vehicle. He was dazed, but was not physically injured. The two other vehicle crew members had been wounded by shrapnel; one of them, Corporal D, was in a serious condition. Illuminated by the burning vehicle, and under sustained and accurate enemy fire directed at and around their position, the three soldiers immediately took what little cover was available. Corporal D was discovered to have sustained life-threatening wounds. The other two soldiers immediately began applying basic first aid. Lance Corporal Apiata assumed command of the situation, as he could see that his superior's condition was deteriorating rapidly.

By this time, however, Lance Corporal Apiata's exposed position, some 70 metres in front of the rest of the Troop, was coming under increasingly intense enemy fire. Corporal D was now suffering serious arterial bleeding and was lapsing in and out of consciousness.

Lance Corporal Apiata concluded that his comrade urgently required medical attention, or he would likely die. Pinned down by the enemy, in the direct line of fire between friend and foe, he also judged that there was almost no chance of such help reaching their position. As the enemy pressed its attack towards Lance Corporal Apiata's position, and without thought of abandoning his colleague to save himself, he took a decision in the highest order of personal courage under fire. Knowing the risks involved in moving to open ground, Lance Corporal Apiata decided to carry Corporal D single-handedly to the relative safety of the main Troop position, which afforded better cover and where medical treatment could be given. He ordered his other colleague, Trooper E, to make his own way back to the rear.

In total disregard of his own safety, Lance Corporal Apiata stood up and lifted his comrade bodily. He then carried him across the 70 metres of broken, rocky and fire swept ground, fully exposed in the glare of battle to heavy enemy fire and into the face of returning fire from the main Troop position. That neither he nor his colleague were hit is scarcely possible. Having delivered his wounded companion to relative shelter with the remainder of the patrol, Lance Corporal Apiata re-armed himself and rejoined the fight in counter-attack. By his actions, he removed the tactical complications of Corporal D's predicament from considerations of rescue.

The Troop could now concentrate entirely on prevailing in the battle itself. After an engagement lasting approximately 20 minutes, the assault was broken up and the numerically superior attackers were routed with significant casualties, with the Troop in pursuit. Lance Corporal Apiata had thereby contributed materially to the operational success of the engagement. A subsequent medical assessment confirmed that Corporal D would probably have died of blood loss and shock, had it not been for

Lance Corporal Apiata's selflessly courageous act in carrying him back to the main Troop lines, to receive the immediate treatment that he needed.

CHAPTER FOURTEEN

MENTOR IN TRAINING

Following his second tour in Afghanistan, and before the day he found out he was to receive the Victoria Cross – and the sky fell on him – Willie Apiata got to lead what passes in the case of an SAS Group member for a normal life. That meant hard work and lots of it.

To keep up he had to keep fit. On selection and cycle, Willie had set a breakneck pace, proving himself one of the faster runners on his cycle, despite his smoking habit. Several years on, the racehorse has become a plodder, more steady and strong than sleek and swift. When he went to Afghanistan he weighed 95 kilos. On his return he was 115.

An overlooked part of the Afghan experience, arduous though it was, was the opportunities it gave Willie to eat, especially when the lamb's tongues and corned beef kept coming to supplement his rations. Travelling in vehicles, rather than on foot, did not help, especially as lack of exercise did not diminish anyone's appetite. When they stopped, a feed could be organised and disposed of in 20 minutes. If they had spent more time in camp, they might have used up some of it training and keeping fit. That said, as events had shown, Willie was fit enough.

On his return to New Zealand and to work, he had to do his biannual Required Fitness Level test. The minimum acceptable standard was two and a half kilometres in 10 minutes. Willie was unusually aware of his whole body as he made his way through this on legs that felt and moved like lead. He finished with just two seconds to spare, and was left bent double, throwing up from the effort. He next managed 30 press-ups – an excellent number considering the extra weight he was having to lift off the ground.

It was the hardest fitness test he had ever done. Failure would have meant no small amount of embarrassment, and two weeks to get into shape and do the test again. Anyone who cannot achieve it is regarded as non-operational, a fate not worth thinking about. At that level of fitness, or lack of it, they can be a danger to themselves and others. SAS self-discipline kicks in about now, and no one fails twice. But try as he might, there is a difference between what a man can do in his twenties and what he can do in his thirties. The older man has to work that much harder to keep up, especially in a highly competitive environment such as the SAS.

During this time, Willie had opportunities to study and gain a variety of qualifications which might be useful both outside and inside the unit. For someone who left school at 15, it was a great chance to add to his skill base. When not on operations, an SAS member also practises basic skills – competitively, of course. No one orders the men to do these things. They are their own best motivators, however, the training is very structured, and has strict competency-based deliverables. The troops have access to numerous shooting ranges for different kinds of target practice. A group may be required to be tested by using some MOE to make entry into the tyre house, for instance.

These daily activities are not without risk, but risk is part of the job. Trust is also part of the job, and a member has to be able to rely on his comrades to keep him covered, and keep him safe. Repetition and perfection go hand in hand. If someone has been on a drill and not done as well as they demanded of themselves, they will make sure they get a chance to do it again . . . and again . . . until it is perfect.

At their base, the men can keep themselves occupied all day and every day. The waiting around that can be part and parcel of operations does not occur here. In the field, however, waiting does not mean boredom. Every moment is spent on edge, because no one ever knows when a routine day – or night – will turn into a nasty one. Readiness is all.

Occasionally, too, there will be a special visitor to liven things up.

We were hosting Prince William for a day. He's just a young lad like us, and there were no dignitaries around, so he could be himself. One of the bros took him for a bit of tracking.

He had a mate with him, and they were buzzing when we got him in on a bus exercise. The scenario was that the bus was full of terrorists and we had to get in there and deal to them. We dressed the Prince and his mate up in our black counter-terrorist gear and gave them some guns.

We made his protection officer, who was ex-SAS himself, part of the enemy group on the bus. We went in and forced him into the aisle and I stood on him. When he got out, he was walking around with my size 11s imprinted on his front, and he kept asking which of us had stood on him, because we had been wearing our masks. When he found out it was me, he said, 'That was awesome – it's been ages since someone has come and stood on me!'

While I was with Prince William, he said something like, 'When you get your medals' and that he hoped he would be there when I got presented them. I didn't know anything about getting any medal at this stage, and I told him I wasn't fussed about getting one either, because I had just been there with the other boys and we were all doing our job. I wonder if he knew something I didn't because the OC had brought him out and said, 'The Prince wants to meet you.' To this day, I don't know one way or the other what he knew.

Prince William and his group didn't want to leave. I guess it made a change from his normal routine. But everyone has an itinerary, and eventually someone was grabbing him by the elbow, saying, 'You've got to come this way, sir.' I know a bit about what that's like now, too.

Having grown up with so much respect for the knowledge of his elders, and having had a chance to acquire some of that knowledge, Willie was now ready to learn how to become an instructor himself.

During his initial training, because of how things had been ordered and because he had gone off to Afghanistan earlier than expected, he had never been pepper sprayed, and it annoyed the professional in him that his mates had experienced something that he had not. So when he took an Advanced Instructors Course for CQB, he insisted someone spray him so he could know what it felt like.

On reflection, he concluded that eating tear gas, which he had done on an MOE exercise, was preferable. This felt like someone had hit him in the eyes with a hammer. He was nauseous, surprising liquids streamed from his eyes and nose, and he couldn't breathe properly. He wanted to soak his head in water and wash it off but knew that was the worst thing he could do as it would wipe the oily substance in even more. Trial and error revealed the fastest-acting antidote was milk. Normal recovery time was 40 minutes; running milk over the affected area brought relief in seven. But he had done his duty by his mates.

Willie has instructed on tracking courses, assault swimmer courses, and helicopter work. Like his elders before him, he keeps an eye out for soldiers who might have the something extra that makes a good SAS member. But he knows the one thing they can't be taught is to want it badly enough. As a trainer, Willie also looks out for anyone who could be reckless or foolhardy. These are weaknesses that show up quickly in training. No one wants someone like that standing next to them when the going gets rough.

He is not a bawling-out kind of instructor. In fact, he is alongside his men every step of the way. If they are being punished, he will do the same punishment they do. He will sprint up that hill carrying the pack, or do the 20 press-ups. He will be the guy demonstrating that a big part of the job is standing shoulder to shoulder with the person next to you – in any conceivable situation.

I've done my Dive Safety Officers course, and I've therefore assisted the trainee dive safety officers doing their course as they instruct the guys who got badged the year before and are out there now getting their advanced skill. When you're a student, you learn the basic skills of being amphibian. And when you do the DSO course, you have to learn a lot more than the students. You have to know the subject you're teaching inside out, so that you can answer any questions you're asked.

I find that as I've progressed with instructing and teaching, I've had to know heaps more. When you do your course to become a basic trainer for tracking, your mind and your eyes get burnt out from interpreting everything you see on the ground. There are so many minute things that say so much. There's so much information to absorb. I'm lucky again, because so much I did in my early life is relevant now. I tell my hunter mates they don't realise they're tracking, just in a different sense.

Even my sales experience is relevant to what I do now. When you're instructing people, you're selling yourself. People have to trust you to take you seriously when they're learning from you, just the same as they have to trust you when they're buying from you. The product is good, but if you're not good too, they won't buy it.

When you're selling a vacuum, you demonstrate all the major parts, how it works, this is what it does, how you use it, what it costs. When you're instructing recruits in the force with a weapon, it's exactly the same. You demonstrate how it works, what it's used for, what it can and can't do. The difference is no one asks how much the weapon costs, because they know it costs heaps.

I was doing a GPMG course once, back when I was a private, and they needed a second in command to fill in. My mate told me I had to go back to the camp to do it. I walked into the barrack room and said, 'Where's your gear?' They said, 'It's all here.' I told them to get the rest of their equipment and I would meet them in five minutes.

They were grabbing their stuff and shooting out the door like madmen. I wondered what the hell was going on. When I got to the top they were waiting for me and looking terrified.

My mate was around the corner cracking up, and I got the truth out of him. Before I had got there he'd said to these guys: 'Do you know who your two-i-c is?'

'No.'

'It's that fella Willie Apiata. He hates privates.'

He'd really put the wind up them before I turned up.

'Listen,' I explained, when I finally found out, 'I'm a private, so I can't hate you and myself at the same time.'

One thing you can be sure of when instructing is that things will always go wrong when you least expect them to. Once we were doing some training in a commercial building in downtown Auckland, working in the elevator shafts to practise rappelling. We needed to go down in the service elevator to pick up some gear. We got in and pushed the button for the floor we wanted to go to.

The elevator made an awful noise and away it went, far too fast. We hit the brakes. We didn't know what the hell was going on. Then it made its noise again and went back up and came to a sudden stop. Then it went back down again. I hit the button to open the doors and it went down some more and then it stopped. I didn't have a clue what was going on. The elevator took off again, and kept going back and forth – four or five floors at a time – for half an hour.

There's someone who comes in from the elevator company to shut things down when we go in there to train, so that it's all safe. We got hold of him and eventually we could hear the elevator doors opening above us. He took us down to the next floor and we got off.

I love working in the shafts, but that time, I kept thinking, 'All we need is for something to break and we're done for.'

Rappelling and other TV-friendly aspects of training were filmed for the ground-breaking documentary series *First Among Equals*, which followed SAS recruits through selection and cycle. Willie's Commanding Officer had inherited the unfinished project from his predecessor. It had been commissioned and produced to meet externally directed requirements to tell a story about an organisation that had enjoyed just over 50 years of near-total anonymity. And it was revolutionary for the amount of insight it gave into the Group's routines with 'behind the scenes' footage, even if everyone's faces were blurred.

One of those faces belonged to Willie Apiata. Like most others in the unit, he had been suspicious when a crew of a) strangers with b) cameras turned up, apparently to follow their every move. The shift from virtual anonymity to a relative degree of exposure was one of the biggest changes in the Group's half-century of existence. But the men accepted their boss's word that this was for the good of the unit. Nothing is done for the unit that isn't good for the individuals within it – just as nothing is permitted to happen to an individual unless it's also good for the unit. They didn't hold back when it came to doing their stuff for the camera.

The film-makers had accepted numerous conditions, including a prohibition on showing the men's faces. They regretted not being able to show Willie's face. As they looked through their rushes, with his wild, bushy hair and unmissable charisma, he would have stood out as every inch the warrior who represented the SAS ideals. But although a lot of footage featuring Willie couldn't be used, because the camera kept being drawn to his face, it didn't matter. All too soon he'd be spending more than enough time in the spotlight.

Sometimes, even a man as driven and devoted to his mission as Willie Apiata needs to get away for awhile. For this, there was and is the family's bush hideaway, 'The Land'. An attachment to the land in general runs deep in Willie's veins. He has spent many days around Te Kaha following old trails and streams, rivers and ranges, getting to know the area footstep by footstep. He is seldom happier than when on his own in the bush, a refuge that has become increasingly important to him as the years have gone by. It is to here he retreats as often as possible.

The East Coast is a remote part of New Zealand, and The Land is in a remote part of the coast. There is almost nothing man-made on this pristine patch of the country. A shed has been built for his mum to sleep in. But for the rest of the family, kitchen, living room and bedroom are all under the stars. For hot water or cooking, there is an old but functional coal range, out in the open and good enough to bake bread on; and Willie has rigged up an outdoor shower, with a plastic sheet to provide some privacy.

The family may not have built on The Land, but they have improved the site. When they started coming here, blackberry was rife. Willie did battle with his chainsaw, and there was much clearing of weeds and overgrowth to be done before anyone could sit back with a beer to enjoy the surroundings. But, as his mum says, this is not a family of procrastinators.

There is an old puriri tree, and there are kereru – which Willie is not allowed to eat.

This is where everything else can be left behind. Emotional turmoil, work stress, worries about partners or children – all vanish into thin, pure air. In summer, the family will stay for weeks at a time, living off the land in every sense, eating what they catch in the bush or from the water. The other name for The Land is 'Camp Running Smooth'.

Usually a week here is all the time out Willie needs, but in 2006 he decided he needed to take a longer break from the SAS, so he spent six months redeployed in Waiouru. No one was happier about this posting than his old training staff sergeant, George, who grabbed him for a training role in the support section of the Officer Cadet School.

George also took the opportunity, in consultation with Willie's SAS CO, to put Willie on a Section Commanders Course, which was something he needed to do to move up the ranks. To many people's surprise, as Willie had not shown much interest in that sort of progress before, he topped the course. Another who once topped that course, and whose name is on the trophy Willie received for doing so, is Defence Force chief Lieutenant General Jerry Mateparae.

Rank does not matter to Willie the way it does to some in the forces. He did not join to become an officer. He joined to become a soldier. He was happy to be a private until he finally joined the SAS, although he had been a senior private and functioned as second in command on occasion. Later he was promoted to lance corporal. Nor does he respect rank for its own sake, being quite capable, when a private, of putting corporals in their place if he knew they had made a mistake. The main error, in his book, was treating your own men badly. This was the same Willie Apiata who did the punishment he gave his men rather than standing back and watching them.

As he saw it, in the Army as in the civilian world, promotion took you further away from what you loved about your job in the first place. You were 'promoted' from a rifle to a computer, slowly being pushed out of the field and into an office. The role of 'Chief Administration Dude' had no appeal. It carried more responsibility and different kinds of challenges, but they were not challenges he felt he needed to pit himself against.

Waiouru was great. I played a season of rugby for the local team. And at work I was under my old trainer, George. It was like going from the 100 kilometre speed limit to the 50 kilometre zone. In the unit we're trying to maintain full speed all the time and it was good to take your foot off the pedal and cruise along for a while. At the end I went back refreshed and ready for action. Instead, I got a Victoria Cross.

One of the best bits was an officer cadet exercise I participated in. We'd been having contacts with guys all day, bumping them in the bush. It was a cross-country exercise and the other party were waiting in one of the old harbours. We had an idea where they were, which was not too far away. We were the enemy.

We were sitting there and one of their guys was looking for one of the officers, and he came walking out.

'You haven't seen Major such and such, have you?' he said.

'Oh no, we haven't, mate, but you know who we are, eh?' I said.

'Yeah, the enemy.'

'You better come over here and sit down.'

'Oh damn.'

He walked over and sat down. I asked him if he smoked.

'Yeah.'

'Have a cigarette then. But the rules are, you're gagged and tied and you can't speak, so if you see your mates come out, say nothing.'

'Oh yeah, no worries.'

On the one hand he was pleased he was having a cigarette, and on the other he was annoyed because he was captured. Pretty soon we heard sounds coming from the bush. The boys and I walked over and we could hear the sound of a little army shovel digging into the ground. I realised someone was planning to have a comfort stop.

I waited till he was nearly ready, and we rushed out of the bush. I walked over and grabbed his gun and his webbing.

'Finish off what you're doing, mate, and then you'll come in with the other boys.'

'I don't want to go now.'

So he came along and we sat him down next to his mate.

'Do you smoke? Here's a cigarette. You're the same as him, though – you're gagged and tied up and you can't speak if you see your friends, okay?'

I realised that since they now had two guys who hadn't come back, there would soon be a search party, so I told our boys to get into position.

I got one of them to crawl into this pig fern. Unless you put your head underneath it, there would be no way you could see anybody. It's perfect camouflage. He crawled out there, and we sat where we were.

We weren't really hiding, but we had our prisoners in plain view when the search party came along. They saw their mates and didn't get it. Their mates sat there looking at them, not saying anything, and smoking their cigarettes, like I had told them. And as the search party came up they walked right past the bro in the pig fern.

He stood up and said: 'Don't move.'

Before you knew it, we had six guys prisoner. I rolled all the smokers cigarettes, because they didn't have any on them. And they were brassed off.

We had a nice group of prisoners, a nice pile of weapons, and all their webbing. I knew that sooner or later there would be an attack when the rest came looking for their mates.

Then George turned up.

'What's going on here, boys?' he said. 'Prisoners?'

'Yeah.'

'Do you need a hand?'

'Yeah. There's a pile of guns here, help yourself.'

He grabbed a machine gun and a whole lot of magazines. I told our boys to get in their firing position.

Sure enough, the other party came pushing through the bush, waiting to be contacted. I had the boys I had stationed in depth open up first, and it was a great battle.

We had a couple of other guys hiding in the pig fern and I told them, 'You're going to get killed pretty quickly, but don't spring up until these fellas are right on top of you, so you can wipe out quite a few of them first.'

Sure enough, the enemy started going for the two guys who were furthest away, and as they pushed forward the bros in the pig fern got up and took out a whole heap of them. One of them even managed to extract himself out of there and continued to battle on.

While all this shooting was going on, I was hiding inside a big tree with roots that formed a small, half-moon cave. Suddenly a gun poked around the corner and pushed forward a little bit in front of me. I reached around and grabbed it by the barrel, and a man came around with it, because he had his sling on. I thought, 'This is good!'

'You're dead, mate,' I said and grabbed his weapon, chucked it away and stayed where I was.

Soon enough another one appeared and pushed forward a bit more. He had his sling on as well, and when I ripped him around the side, he ended up lying on top of his mate.

After that, I came out and joined the firefight and we near wiped out their whole platoon. There weren't many of them left. But in the end, everyone in the enemy party had to die, and we all fell on the ground so they could finish off their thing.

This was a worthwhile exercise and everybody learnt a lot. And after all, these guys were training to be officers and at the end of their one year or two years that is what happens – they graduate as officers and get to be in charge of platoons.

I was trying to make it interesting for the cadets. I wanted to give them a bit of realism. I really challenged those guys. I think they got a bit extra out of me, because I tried to get them to think and work harder.

When I was at Waiouru I learnt another lesson about logistics. George had given me some thunder flashes, like big double happies, that you use to simulate grenades. You strike them and throw them. You're meant to do it one at a time, but I could get several going and throw them all. By mid-afternoon I started to run out, but when I tried to see about getting some more, George told me the ones I had were supposed to last me a week!

There was another explosion about to go off in Willie's vicinity. His Troop Commander in Afghanistan had made good on his promise to nominate him for a bravery award. He filled in New Zealand Defence Force Form Md592, 'Nomination for New Zealand Honours and Awards'. There is a box on that form for the Victoria Cross for New Zealand, but the one ticked for Willie was the one beneath that – for the New Zealand Gallantry Star. The form went to his OC, then his CO, who sent it to the Land Component Commander, who approved it and sent it to the Chief of Army, who approved it and sent it, in 2004, to the then Defence Force chief Air Marshal Bruce Ferguson.

Ferguson had been in Afghanistan not long after the contact and heard about it with interest. He thought it possible Willie's actions might merit more than the Gallantry Star, so he consulted a lot of people and collected as many accounts of what had happened as he could. He also sought advice from overseas. Eventually a recommendation went to the Minister of Defence, Phil Goff, and Goff passed it on to the Prime Minister, Helen Clark. But, as had always been the case, the award of the Victoria Cross itself could only be made, on the PM's recommendation, by the monarch. The Prime Minister made such a recommendation to the Queen.

CHAPTER FIFTEEN

WILLIE APIATA, VC

Paradoxically, at the point where he became universally recognised as a man of action, Willie almost disappears from his own story. How the news that he had been awarded a Victoria Cross was broken to him, and to the rest of the world, had been arranged and planned by others. In some cases, they had been working behind the scenes on this announcement for months. He did not have to do anything. He was simply the pivot around which other people revolved.

Willie had made an appointment to see his Commanding Officer on the morning of Monday 2 July 2007 to discuss various matters. Unusually, when he had asked the OC if he could make the appointment, the OC had told Willie he could see the CO at nine on Monday, without consulting the CO himself.

I thought, 'There's something fishy going on here.'

I was put on group orderly for 10 days. That means you're on sentry every night. Even when there's no one else here, there is always a presence inside the compound. That weekend, it was me.

There was a big function on the Saturday with the band and a lot of getting on the juice. I was up in my hut when a mate came up. No one ever comes to see you on group orderly.

'What's going on?' I said.

'I just came to see you. Are you all right?'

'I'm fine – happy as I ever am to be in here on group orderly on the weekend.'

Later, on Sunday morning, I was lying on the bed in my boxers watching the monitors, when the RSM put his head in the door. 'Get your gear together,' said the RSM. 'Get dressed, go down to the carving and wait there until the CO is ready to have a meeting.'

'Today?' I said. 'It's not supposed to be till Monday.'

'No, the boss wants to do it now while he is in at work,' he said, and that was that. The replacement was there ready and waiting to take over from me. I realised later they hadn't wanted me to go home, and that was part of why I was on group orderly. That way they'd know where I was every minute. I had been spewing about it, because I wasn't rostered on. I was a lamb to the slaughter.

When I was going to the office, I thought I must have some other task to do on base. Often, if there wasn't a driver you might have to go to the airport and pick somebody up. Then when I walked in I saw those three envelopes on the table, each with my name on. There was one from the Governor-General, one from the Prime Minister and one from the Minister of Defence.

The boss told me to open the first one.

How do you explain what you're feeling? I didn't want to read any more after the first one. I was the first of the boys who were there to find out.

I asked the CO when my mate who was injured would find out. He said, when the rest of the boys find out. The next thing I said was that I was only doing my job. The last thing anyone wanted was a medal. We did the rap and we were lucky to be still alive.

The Governor-General, Anand Satyanand, wrote:

> I am delighted to inform you that Her Majesty The Queen has awarded you the Victoria Cross for New Zealand (the VC) for an act of most conspicuous gallantry in saving the life of your comrade under enemy fire, whilst on operations in Afghanistan in 2004. I read your citation with great interest. The honour that has been bestowed on you by Her Majesty is, in my view, richly deserved. I understand that yours is the first VC to be awarded to a New Zealander since the end of World War II, and is the first such award to a serving member of the SAS anywhere in the Commonwealth.
>
> Your award will be announced in a special honours list on the morning of Monday 2 July 2007. I would be grateful if this information could remain confidential until then.

Willie would have liked it to remain confidential forever.

He read the next letter, which was from the Prime Minister, Helen Clark, commending him on the award. Then he read the third letter, from Minister of Defence Phil Goff, congratulating him.

Then he looked at his boss. His mind was going a hundred miles an hour, trying first to accept what has happening and then process some of the implications of having his life irrevocably changed. And he had a hundred questions.

'You're going to out me, aren't you?' he said. As uncomfortable as he would find that, he knew that the magnitude of the award meant there was no way of avoiding his name becoming known to the public.

'Yes, I am, Willie,' said the CO, 'but you must understand this medal will confer great responsibility on you but it will also bring great opportunity and great privilege and we must balance those three things.'

If there were too many opportunities – which there were – and not enough responsibility, or too much responsibility with no privileges, then there would be problems. Willie would have liked to keep things as low key as possible but then that would conflict with several other requirements. Not just those of the media, the public and politicians, but also those of the unit.

'We've been planning this for some time, so trust us,' said the CO. 'There's a lot of mechanisms in place and the first thing we've got to do is get you decked out appropriately.' And with that, Willie and the team went off to get him a haircut and some new clothes.

You cannot aim for it. You cannot sit a series of qualifying exams for one. And you cannot engineer a situation in which to win it. Few awards carry such mystique as the Victoria Cross.

Established during the Crimean War (1853–56), it is awarded by the monarch to members of the services for bravery in the face of the enemy. It can be awarded to any rank. The first recipients received theirs from Queen Victoria in 1857. The first VCs awarded in New Zealand were won in the New Zealand Wars of the nineteenth century. Approximately half of all VCs were awarded during the First World War. According to enthusiast and collector Lord Michael Ashcroft, it has been estimated that the chance of surviving the sort of action that merits a Victoria Cross is one in 10.

The VCs have been made from melted-down Russian cannons won at Sebastopol during the Crimean War. The rank, name and unit of service of the recipient is engraved on the reverse and the date of the act for which the Cross is awarded is engraved on the central portion of the reverse. In Willie's case, due to the requirement for operational security, his date is engraved as the day of announcement. The medal itself has no value. This was a deliberate choice. When the award was instituted it was feared that, because all ranks were eligible, if the medals were made of precious metal, indigent recipients from the lower orders might melt theirs down and sell them for the price of the material. Like every Victoria Cross ever awarded, Willie's medal would be made by Hancocks Jewellers of London.

As well as being the first Victoria Cross for a New Zealander since the Second World War and the first to a serving SAS member, Willie's award was notable for several other reasons.

It was the first Victoria Cross for New Zealand, the most auspicious of the four New Zealand Gallantry Awards instituted by royal warrant in 1999: 'For most conspicuous gallantry, or some daring or pre-eminent act of valour or self-sacrifice or extreme devotion to duty in the presence of the enemy or of belligerents.'

In addition, Willie is one of only 13 living recipients of the VC, which has been won by 21 New Zealanders – twice by Charles Upham. He is the only living New Zealand recipient, one of only 14 in the world since the Second World War, and the only New Zealander within that period. He is only the third Maori recipient after William Rhodes-Moorhouse and Moananui-a-Kiwa Ngarimu. With Ngarimu, he is one of two recipients from the East Coast, and he is one of only two still serving in the military.

Willie's award also has a connection to one of the very first VCs. The deed that earned that one, as described in Michael Ashcroft's book *Victoria Cross Heroes*, uncannily echoes Willie's. During an action of the Crimean War, boatswain's mate Henry Curtis could see from his trench a soldier sitting up and calling for help. With three others, he ran across 70 yards of no-man's-land under heavy fire to rescue the wounded man and carry him to safety. Willie traversed the same distance under heavy fire to carry a wounded comrade to safety.

Willie was well aware of Victoria Cross traditions. Learning about them had formed part of his training. If it took him some time to get his thoughts straight, part of the reason was that he knew that one of the things the award could mean was turmoil. The VC is one of those things that can wreak either great good or great harm. It can inspire and focus people's drive, but it can also bring out greed and venality. It is capable of dividing families and even nations. Some have buckled under the strain of attention that accompanies it. Past winners have fallen victim to alcoholism and poverty. When you have a VC, you never have to buy a drink.

Other New Zealanders had struggled with the award. When Upham's bar was announced and the media began to gather, he first locked himself in his bathroom, then climbed out the window and ran to a neighbour's house to elude them. Another recipient, Keith Elliot, described the attention he received as 'an ordeal for which I was unprepared'.

When the RSM told Willie that plans for his VC had been under way for some time, he was not exaggerating. The CO had learnt the award was in the pipeline when he had taken on the position 10 months previously. He knew this would have to be handled so as to cover off innumerable contingencies. It was good news. It could go brilliantly well. But there were plenty of ways in which it could go wrong.

Willie would be prepared. From August 2006, when the award was still only a nomination, until it was confirmed in April 2007, the CO spent an inordinate amount of time working on what became known as Operation Moose. Nearer the time of the announcement there were discussions with other senior-level defence personnel. A plan was put in place that fell into three parts: the man, the medal, the unit.

The first priority was the man. There is a saying in the SAS – the man is the regiment, the regiment is the man. It was clear to the CO and to Army PR adviser Dave Courtney that the media – and Willie's relations with them – would be crucial. There would be a public thirst for information about an unknown corporal named Willie Apiata, and that information would have to be carefully managed. If the Army didn't manage it, someone else would try to and do it badly. So a reluctant hero was born.

The next priority for the SAS was the medal, which also needed to be well looked after. It had to be treated in a way commensurate with the dignity and respect that should be associated with a VC and a VC holder, as well as those who had gone before and the very institution it represents. It was, in every sense, Willie's VC, to do with whatever he wished. But deciding what to do with their medals had created problems for many holders in the past. The metal of which it is comprised was not of any worth, but the medal itself was. It was not just an accessory. It was an item of national significance.

And the third priority was the unit, which would have a lot of attention focused upon it. It still had core business to undertake that had nothing to do with the Victoria Cross. The SAS had just got over starring in a TV series – now it had this bombshell to contend with.

This was new territory for everybody concerned. The fact it was the first Victoria Cross for New Zealand meant no one had ever won exactly this award, and the last time a New Zealander had won a Victoria Cross the world was a very different place. Media were far less pervasive; the line between public and private figures was much more clearly defined; the public had different expectations of their heroes; defence units were not in the business of preparing long-term PR plans. In those days it was not necessary to have an online media kit available to accompany announcements. At Staff College the CO's training had included two days on public relations. He has learnt a lot more since July 2007.

There were no experts to go to for advice on exactly this situation, but there were numerous wise heads to consult, and the elite NZSAS command team was used to thinking innovatively and reacting to and dealing quickly with unprecedented demands in dangerous situations. That was what the SAS was set up to do. Lawyers were found to give Willie advice. It was also clear he would need someone to act as a manager – to advise him and liaise with the rest of the world just like any other public personality's manager.

However, unlike the case with other celebrities, this award and the notice it brought would not be the stepping stone to increased income and the dubious benefits of public recognition for either Willie or a manager. Nor did it offer anything in the way of opportunities to maximise a managerial income. It was not a stepping stone to anything of that kind. The person in this position would need to understand how the unit worked and appreciate its ethos and values. Willie asked his CO to take on the job.

A lot of decisions had been made for Willie already. Much of the planning had been done with the superlative level of subterfuge that could be expected from the Special Air Service. Defence public relations people had been brought up from Wellington a few days before the announcement and sent out on the range where Willie was doing some shooting to get a sense of the man. He was pointed out to them and they got talking. Willie thought they were asking a lot of questions, but he had no idea why they were there and, anyway, he was used to people being nosy about his job.

On the Sunday he was informed, Courtney had also done internet and White Pages® searches on the name Apiata, knowing media would trawl these for contacts with information on Willie. He showed Willie the list and got him to identify any who were relatives. All under control.

There was a film crew on hand the day Willie was informed about his award. The CO had rung Desert Road Productions, makers of the *First Among Equals* documentary series, and told them it would be worth their while to be in attendance at Rennie Lines that Sunday morning. They would be present on and off for nearly a year, following Willie to make the acclaimed documentary *Reluctant Hero*. It made things a lot easier for everyone, especially the subject, that Willie had become accustomed to having cameras around during the making of the previous doco.

A little-known SAS tradition is that during his time a Commanding Officer can elect to commission a work of art. Willie's CO had been thinking of commissioning a sculpture of a tracker so took advantage of this tradition to arrange for one to be made of Willie, who was a qualified tracker. He got Willie's OC to make him pose in his Afghan gear, with another unit member, for what Willie was told might become an artwork. He noticed that a lot of photos were being taken of him, not so many of his mate.

The CO also put someone in place to be Willie's mentor. The right mentor had to have both experience and Willie's respect. It was not a role the CO could fill because he was also Willie's boss. It needed to be someone outside the command chain, who Willie could unload to and think things over with, and was wise enough to stand aside and let him make his own decisions. He asked Sam, the officer who had overseen Willie in training and who Willie had been so delighted to see on the ground when he got to Afghanistan. Sam said he would be happy to take on the role – but only if Willie was happy about it too. He was.

One thing the SAS has never lacked is people with experience, and to Willie, Sam was like the Bible – a source of all the answers you could ever need. He has been with the unit more than 30 years, an unusually long time. Teacher is one of his primary roles, and he would be of crucial assistance to his charge in the months to come. He seldom told Willie what he thought he should do but listened and encouraged him while Willie talked, as his thoughts nearly always led him to the right decision.

As far as Sam was concerned, the history began at letter opening minus 10 minutes. That's when he started shooting a home video that would record much of the next few weeks. In the video, during the moments before Willie arrives at the CO's office, there is a palpable air of tension in the offices at Rennie Lines. Willie opening the first envelope would be like the moment a parachutist steps out of a plane. All the planning has been done, but no one knows exactly where he is going to land, and it's too late to get back on.

Sam followed Willie back to his room, which was in a state of mild chaos, normal housekeeping duties having been put to one side while he was on group orderly. He kept filming.

'Still trying to sink in, really,' says Willie to the camera. 'It's only been a couple of hours since I found out and I still don't really know what's hit me. The person I'm most afraid to tell would be my partner, because I'm not going to be home tomorrow. I'm going to get an earful ...'

CHAPTER SIXTEEN

CELEBRITY

Things started to move at bewildering speed. Over the next few days numerous people would hear the name of Willie Apiata for the first time. And many of those in his immediate circle would see a very different man from the one they knew. He had to learn how to be Willie Apiata, VC. He would do it by being himself, which is not always easy under pressure, especially when that pressure comes from the media. But it was easier for Willie than it might have been for other people, because he had a very clear idea who he was.

On Sunday evening, Willie, his Commanding Officer, now official mentor Sam and the RSM flew to Wellington. He was fitted for a new uniform. At Defence House, he met Defence Force chief Lieutenant

General Jerry Mateparae, Mateparae's predecessor Bruce Ferguson, who had been a prime mover in the award of the VC, and Defence Minister Phil Goff, whom he'd met previously in Afghanistan, when Goff visited and Willie was one of those who guided him on the tour. And he received a PR briefing: Willie would be made available to the media at 2 p.m. on Monday. It was all so simple. It would also be the most terrifying experience of his life.

The next morning, there would be more PR and media advice, and in the nick of time. Willie would finally be allowed to tell his partner. At 10 a.m. his colleagues back in Auckland would be told of his award at the same time as the Prime Minister was making the official announcement in Wellington.

The CO could have added a fourth item to his list of VC priorities: the man, the medal, the unit . . . the family. He knew from other VC winners' experience what kind of pressure they would come under. He had an obligation to ensure they were looked after during this process too. They had to be kept informed about what was going on, and protected where necessary from unwelcome intrusion into their lives. After all, they weren't the ones getting the medal or the recognition, apart from acknowledgement that together they formed a close and remarkable family who had produced a remarkable man.

SAS men were sent down country to be ready near the family when the announcement was made. One would look after Willie's partner in Whakatane, the other went to Opotiki to be with his mother and sisters. Willie was not allowed to tell them until half an hour before the world was told. However, he had warned his mum that he might be getting a promotion from lance corporal to corporal, so she knew at least one good thing was in the air for her son. On Monday morning she was at work in the orchard when he rang.

'You need to go home now,' Willie told her. 'Someone is going to meet you and he will tell you all about it.'

When she was home, he called again and was finally able to get the message across. Her heart was fit to burst with pride, but she was used to being proud of her only son. She would tell people, when they inevitably said, 'You must be so proud of your boy', that she was proud of all her children. Any mother would say that, but she meant it. Without so much as two days' PR training she said exactly the right things: 'Wills has always been a hero in our eyes. He was famous long before the VC came along. He's always been our man.'

In Opotiki, Willie's eldest sister finished her early-morning work and went to visit her younger sister. She was a little surprised to see her mother there at that hour talking to a man whom she took to be, from his conservative attire and grooming, a Jehovah's Witness. (Not everyone in the SAS looks like Willie.)

It was just as well the Group member was wearing a suit rather than his Army gears, because anyone with a relation in the Group who has a man in uniform turn up unannounced on their doorstep will automatically assume the worst. But his sister was no wiser about who he was or why he was there. Their mother came inside.

'I'm not going to be long,' she said to the girls. 'I'm going with this guy and I'll be back soon.'

'All right, okay. We'll sit here.'

After a while she rang and told the girls to make sure they both sat tight. She was calling from a pub, which was extremely unusual. Willie's mum was not a hit-the-pub-at-10 a.m.-on-Monday kind of person. But the SAS man had realised that having a few beers on hand might help keep everyone together for the rest of the day, so they had stopped to pick up a couple of boxes. Eventually, his mum returned and told her daughters that their brother had been awarded the Victoria Cross for New Zealand. There was much yelling and jumping in the air and they followed reports of the announcement on TV all day long. Unable to hug Willie in person, they stroked the set every time he appeared.

Defence PR people were also on hand to tell them what to expect. They had to inform them that, as much as they would want to be with their brother, they wouldn't be able to see him for some time. He was public property now. They would have to get used to little things, such as the fact they were no longer known by their name, but as 'the VC's sisters'. And to big things, like intrusive newspaper stories, errors published about the family, and strangers thinking they knew all about them. But, like Willie, they knew who they were, and didn't depend on other people's opinions to feel good about themselves.

The day after the announcement, Willie's family received some extra PR advice from the Defence Force's Dave Courtney. He explained how the trespass laws worked relevant to where journalists could and could not go to speak to them. He told them that whatever happened they mustn't lose their temper because such an explosion would be repeated ad nauseam in news stories. He reminded them that anything they did could follow them – and Willie – around for the rest of their lives. By way of consolation, he opened his laptop, went to the *New Zealand Herald* website and showed them pages of laudatory comments from readers responding to the story about Willie's award. He reminded them that if things ever went sour or they got down, they could go online, read these and remind themselves how proud the whole country was of their boy.

The man. The medal. The unit also had to be told. For them, as for the family, the award of a VC was the last thing they were expecting.

Everyone had known Willie was due some distinction for valour for what he had done that night in Afghanistan – particularly those who had also been there – but they little suspected he would receive the highest such award in the Commonwealth.

Because he had to be in Wellington with Willie, and because he acknowledged that these men were stakeholders in all this as well, the Commanding Officer had recorded a video address. The whole Group was assembled, which is a very rare event. A cover story had been invented for the occasion about the CO needing everyone together because he was unhappy with some aspect of accounting for stores. Some of the more imaginative men anticipated this was going to be The Big One. They were to be deployed in a major operation. Their minor disappointment that such was not the case was more than made up for by their happiness on Willie's behalf when the CO announced his award. There was a sharp intake of breath, which the PR person present thought probably marked an extreme of emotion for SAS members.

One or two journalists had sniffed something in the air. In a rare case of journalists and SAS thinking alike, they had rung and asked Defence PR if the unit was about to be deployed, because they had heard there was something big coming up involving the Group. Meanwhile, the Defence media team had the opposite of the traditional PR nightmare to contend with. But good news can be as complicated as bad – especially when the person at the heart of the story is temperamentally disinclined to being the centre of media attention.

Willie was an intelligent man who could think and speak for himself. The main message the PR advisers had to get through to him was that he would have to answer questions. People would want to know things about him because he had performed a remarkable feat.

And he would have to give them information. There was a rehearsal interview with the PR team to help him prepare. Willie had two default reactions to questions: 'Do I have to talk about this?' and 'I don't want to talk about that.' Even in rehearsal he was fiercely stony-faced. There was nothing to smile about, as he saw it, and his monosyllabic approach was perfectly strategised.

'How do you feel in the company of Upham and other VC winners?'

'Don't know.'

'Too soon to tell?'

'Yes.'

'Does it give you goose bumps?'

'I haven't even had the chance to think that far ahead. I'm still trying to get used to what's actually happened.'

'Were you aware of the history of the VC?'

'Yes.'

'You know these guys have done some heroic acts. Let's talk about the act and go back to the night. The citation tells a bit of the story. I'll go through it to refresh your memory, though you probably don't need that.'

The interviewer read from the citation.

'All that noise erupted around you – what was your thought then?'

'Where's my mate?'

...

'The citation is accurate and factual and what you read there is what happened.'

'You're uncomfortable talking about the night?'

'Because of operational security, there are some aspects that can't be disclosed.'

'What are your thoughts about the future?'

'I'm taking it one day at a time.'

. . .

'You know the word they're going to use to describe you?'

'I understand that.'

'Are you a hero?'

'I'm Willie Apiata.'

All of which was roughly how the real thing went in Defence House with about 30 journalists at two o'clock that Monday afternoon. One difference was that Willie had his CO and the CDF alongside him. On one occasion he deferred to his CO when questions touched on operational matters or when he just wanted someone else to say he was not going to answer a question.

They flew me down to Wellington and then it started. You can have so much preparation but it is still hard. I don't think anyone could prepare themselves for what I walked into that morning.

That was the freakiest thing I have ever done in my life. Every time someone takes a photo, they take a little piece of me. They're capturing me on that side of the lens.

You go in, and you have to pause, waiting for the cameras to stop clicking before you sit down. Then they want to hear me speak, and I'm not much of a public speaker, that's for real. I can take a lesson if it is military orientated, but the general public is a different story.

And the media are the scariest people in the world, because we have never talked to them in the SAS. We know they would love to find out the nuts and bolts of what we get up to. So to go out and actually talk to the buggers, you've got to be very careful what you say.

It was like they didn't know really what to ask me, because they didn't really know me, they didn't know much about me or anything.

Wellington is not my place, so it was walking into foreign territory. You just hope you've got someone watching your back. There's a lot of emotion going through you, and it's hard to talk to people when you're still trying to deal with what you're feeling inside.

'I was doing my job and just looking after my mates,' Willie told the room.

'What was going through your mind at that time?'

'Where's my buddies? How can I help them?'

'You weren't worried about being hit?'

At that question, whatever its merits, Willie looked at the CO, who picked up the cue and said, 'I think it's time to move the questions somewhere else.'

That night Sam was on hand again with his camera. He asked Willie, who was having a beer, how he felt now.

'It's good to be off the dry,' said Willie.

The first stranger to congratulate him was champion cyclist Sarah Ulmer who approached him in an airport lounge. He didn't recognise her but was delighted when he found out who she was.

Soon he was approached and asked for an autograph for the first time. He looked to his CO for permission, received it and wrote 'Willie' on a piece of paper.

'I think we can do a bit better than that,' said the CO.

Now he signs autographs 'William Apiata, VC'.

So much to learn.

Willie breathed a huge sigh of relief when the press conference was over, but it was premature. The media had precious little to go on after his performance, which had not allowed them to gather sufficient material for the big story this kind of event warranted. Defence personnel realised that genuine public interest would not be satisfied by the brief encounter and tried to convince the CO that a few one-on-one interviews later in the week were justified. More than reluctantly, after some lively discussion, Willie's boss saw their point and agreed to a second round of interviews on Friday.

The boss had been reluctant because he knew that, tough as he was, there was only so much of this sort of attention Willie could stand. He wouldn't have thrown a reporter through a window – well, not if anyone was watching – but he would have been able to make his displeasure known in other ways.

Access had to be tightly managed. Willie was slightly more forthcoming being interviewed in his own environment at Rennie Lines and not facing a group. But no one could have doubted that this man had undertaken special training in resistance to interrogation. He liked most of the people, disliked some, noted one interviewer wearing more make-up than he had ever seen on a man before – and that included his own cam paint – and reacted badly when reporters practising the time-honoured trick of getting deep into the subject's personal space got deep into his own personal space. Willie needs more personal space than most people, so it wasn't too hard for them to intrude.

The key to it all was the simple phrase 'I'm Willie Apiata'. When Willie was allowed to be himself, he and the media got on just fine. When they tried to cajole him into being someone else – someone who would reveal more than he was comfortable doing, or was authorised to do – the barriers immediately went up. And if his superiors had tried to train him into being a grinning, glad-handing, media-friendly celebrity, they would have been making the same mistake and achieved the same result – a taciturn, awkward interviewee.

At the end of the week, he was able to go home for the weekend, accompanied by Sam, to discuss things with his partner and the family. After a few days off to go pig hunting, Willie had to face his next duty: preparing for his investiture, and even more public attention.

CHAPTER SEVENTEEN

RELUCTANT HERO

I still don't think that I'm a hero. And it's not easy having people telling you you're one. Some people understand that. I'm proud of what I did – I saved a man's life and that's the best thing that came out of this whole business. None of our boys got killed and we all came home. You can't ask for anything more than that. It took a whole team to get us all out of there, not just one man. We were all heroes on the day, as far as I'm concerned.

People don't realise it's a natural instinct to help someone. Some people may go into shock when they see an unreal thing happen right in front of them, and some people don't. Everybody reacts differently.

You can give a person all the mental tools, but it's up to him which ones he decides to use. The SAS gave us a lot of tools. If you stuck them in a box and tried to drag them around, you wouldn't be able to move.

I've met real heroes all through my life. They are people I look up to because they have showed me something special, but they're just normal people.

My biggest hero would be my mum, and she always will be. She means the world to me. She looked after us all on her own.

But I also look up to all the old fellas during my years growing up who've shown me things. I never had famous heroes, just people I knew.

Like it or not, reluctant or enthusiastic, Willie was now a hero in the eyes of the world – and not just any hero, but a member of the small but select group of 13 living holders of the Victoria Cross. For someone who enjoyed relative anonymity, this was bad enough; for someone whose job had hitherto required him to remain anonymous it went right against the grain. The whole point of his job was that no one knew he did it. Now, anyone would be able to front up to him in the street and ask him about his life and career.

With the exception of his Commanding Officer and the Regimental Sergeant Major – both of whose faces had been seen in the *First Among Equals* documentary series knowing what was to follow – Willie became the first serving NZSAS member who was allowed to be identified. As the Group's joke has it, there are only two kinds of SAS members – pixelated or blacked out.

Willie had gone from an existence in the shadows to life in the spotlight without any period of adjustment. No one could have prepared him for it. They could tell him it was going to happen, and be there to support him, but he was going to have to work out how to deal with the transition himself.

Much of the media coverage had a predictably breathless tone. Some of it made no sense to him – such as his moustache appearing on a list of 21 things for New Zealanders to be happy about: poor New

Zealanders. As far as he was concerned, his moustache was simply something that got trimmed when too much ice cream kept getting stuck in it. It is also a mixed blessing – great for cartoonists, as it makes him instantly recognisable anywhere he goes; but without it, no one knows who he is. He could keep it off to retain his anonymity, but it is his moustache and his face, so why should he?

Willie understood that being interviewed was a necessary evil. He was never going to like it, but he was always going to be polite and helpful and try to say the right thing. It was just another area in which he didn't want to let the boys down.

Any number of highly qualified people who work at the top level of demanding professions can make fools of themselves in a jumble of nerves doing simple radio or TV interviews. There was no reason to expect a soldier from Te Kaha to suddenly turn into a major TV talent. Meeting the media was one thing that never had been – and never would be – included in cycle.

By the same token, many famous people have set out to become so. Others – performers, politicians – know that becoming so will be an important part of getting to the top. But every day, other ordinary people, like Willie, become famous because something they never expected to happen has made them the centre of a news story. His position was not unique, but that didn't make it any easier to handle. Willie simply took recognition as it came.

> Their excellencies the Governor-General of New Zealand, the Hon Anand Satyanand and Susan Satyanand invite [name] to an Investiture Ceremony at Government House, Wellington, at 10.30 a.m. on Thursday 26 July 2007. Dress – Ladies: Day dress – Gentlemen: Lounge suit or uniform.

The whole family went. They had never known such excitement.

His mother and two elder sisters had never flown before, let alone been invited to Government House. They arrived in Wellington the day before and made the most of being put up in a downtown hotel.

The team went out to Government House for a recce – to get the lay of the land, like all good soldiers do. Willie needed to see where everything was going to happen, and work out who would be where – especially the media. That night, he, the CO, Sam and the RSM stayed up to keep the rest of the family company, who were not disposed to have an early night. In the morning there was time for a rare group photo with the whole whanau before heading off to the ceremony. The VC is a proud tradition and the ceremony was proudly traditional.

All the dignitaries and guests assembled: Willie and his family, his SAS comrades, others being awarded medals that day, the Prime Minister Helen Clark, Minister of Defence Phil Goff and Minister of Maori Affairs Parekura Horomia. Other guests included Wilson Whineray, former All Black captain, successful businessman, previous NZSAS Colonel Commandant and an enthusiastic supporter of the unit. Willie's mum was quite at home, not least with Phil Goff, whose family she knew from the old days up north.

A piano version of 'God Save the Queen' resounded in the echoing acoustic of the timber-floored room, with its marble pillars and heavy drapes. The Governor-General and his wife stood on a red-carpeted podium before a large portrait of the Queen hung above two flags. These were surroundings designed to impress and inspire.

Willie was more attentive than relaxed as the Governor-General announced his award: 'As Governor-General, I have the authority and privilege on behalf of Her Majesty the Queen to confer the honour of the Victoria Cross for New Zealand on Corporal Bill Henry Apiata of the New Zealand Special Air Service Group. You are the first person to receive the Victoria Cross for New Zealand.'

Pinning the piece of bronze and its ribbon to Willie's chest, the Governor-General then referred to the wider significance of the event. 'It is a great privilege to share this special New Zealand moment with you,' he said. 'You should wear it with pride.'

His mum and the girls teared up. His young son punctured the solemnity of the occasion with a bit of four-year-old's self-expression. Willie shared a hongi with the Governor-General and the two turned in unison to face the cameras as a small electrical storm of flashes went off. There was a brief, trademark Willie, interview outside for waiting media – 'I'm a man of few words . . .' he said superfluously, and then it was back inside for lunch.

The family left Wellington later that day in their various directions. Willie went back to the unit and had a few beers with the boys – the first official celebration of the award at Rennie Lines. Willie told them: 'I carry it for us bros, the lads who were there that day, the ones who are here now, the ones that have passed and the ones in the future.'

A few days later, Willie, Sam, the RSM, CO and the Victoria Cross set off on a road trip. The itinerary included celebrations for the 50th anniversary of the 1st Battalion, Royal New Zealand Infantry Regiment. As he travelled south, Willie would be reminded that, although the Victoria Cross is no respecter of rank, all ranks respect the VC. He had to crack out more salutes in those few days than he would have done in the previous two years as saluting is not done in the SAS.

My medals got to Waiouru before me. They'd been sent ahead to the military museum to be mounted.

I heard later that while that was going on some kids from my old school,

Te Whanau-a-Apanui, were visiting. Colonel (rtd) Ray Seymour, the museum boss, found out and showed them the medals. They all had their photos taken with them. I liked that.

We had a dinner the night before the official 50th at the sergeants' mess in Waiouru with the Formation Sergeant Major. They said, 'Would you like the demo boys to come along?' I was keen because I spent six months as one of them, and they're a good bunch of dudes from the Territorials.

The RSM, Sam and I stayed in The Homestead, a place that's reserved for VIPs. It's a beautiful building with a lot of history. Every time I've been to Waiouru, we've stayed in the barracks and looked at that building and thought, 'I wonder who stays in that place?' Then I found out it was going to be me. I found the biggest room and said, 'This is mine' and left the others with the single beds.

And the food. The demo boys gave us some kina and I found some beer in the fridge and some scallops in the freezer and cooked them up.

I was standing on the verandah and some of the boys from the barracks went past and yelled out, 'Hey, bro, party at your place?' and I said, 'It's my first time here, bro. I don't want to ruin it!'

On the way to the 50th, the team made a visit to Palmerston North Boys' High School. Willie found the haka from 1400 boys a moving experience and the visit touched him in ways that meant a lot to him, with its meeting of youth and experience, promise and potential fulfilled. He had a lot of respect for the school's history, notably as he looked at the names of old boys who had fallen in previous wars, and the entire school respected his achievement. Many autographs were sought and given. The school's motto: 'Nothing Achieved Without Hard Work' is almost a paraphrase of the SAS's 'Who Dares Wins'.

At the cocktail party that night, 1 RNZIR was presented with copy one of the sculpture of Willie that had been the subject of so much clandestine effort on the CO's behalf prior to the announcement of his award. They were astonished at the apparent speed with which it had been made. And Willie himself had been astonished the first time he saw it, too.

When he was in Wellington, someone had pointed out a bust of another New Zealand VC winner, Lord Freyberg, to him and suggested that soon there would be a similar one of Willie. He little suspected how soon. The commission for a statuette had already been placed. Many people have tried to purchase copies, but they are not for sale. They are far too precious to be sold. One is in the trophy room at Rennie Lines.

At Linton, Willie found giving someone a statuette of himself as a gift too odd, even in a world which had gone quite strange over the previous few weeks. Statues were supposed to be of dead people, and he was very much alive and well. The next time a statuette was presented, the CO would have to do the honours.

So far, Willie had received warm welcomes wherever he'd gone – at Government House, Waiouru, Palmerston North Boys' High and 1 RNZIR. But none of these was anything compared to the reception he would receive when he went home to Te Kaha.

CHAPTER EIGHTEEN

TE KAHA

It was the biggest thing to happen in Te Kaha in anyone's lifetime. The formal homecoming ceremony for Willie Apiata at Tukaki Marae stretched over two days in August 2007 and was one of those rare events that did not just leave everyone feeling satisfied, but exceeded all expectations.

The people of Te Kaha, who boasted another Victoria Cross winner in the person of Moananui-a-Kiwa Ngarimu, were keen to pay tribute to their newly honoured son. Willie regards Te Kaha as home and this marae as his turangawaewae (literally, 'a place to stand'). He treasures his affiliations with Te Whanau-a-Apanui and Ngati Porou, whose marae it is, although officially his blood connection is with the Nga Puhi of the north, many of whom travelled south to attend the homecoming.

Estimates of crowd size that weekend vary from 2000 to 4000. Whatever the exact figure, for a town with a permanent population of around 350, hosting the homecoming was a mammoth endeavour – and one they took to with gusto. The Army, Navy and Air Force combined forces to take care of food, catering and other services, but it was the people of Te Kaha who did most to make the event. They did everything from throwing open their backyards for parking, to contributing mammoth amounts of bread and trifle. Crayfish, mutton birds, oysters, mussels and hangi were also on the menu.

There is a good reason why the word 'welcome' is used to describe what happens when people are brought onto a marae. Among those being welcomed with Willie were numerous whanau, both his immediate family and his Parkinson family, the Prime Minister, the Chief of Defence Force Jerry Mateparae, returned servicemen, past and present SAS men and members of 28 (Maori) Battalion, which was Ngarimu's battalion.

Willie's mum took her customary low-key approach, deferring to the Prime Minister and letting Helen Clark walk next to Willie when he went on to the marae and sit next to him later at lunch. His partner sat on his left. This kept his mum out of the limelight, which is the way she likes it. She was there to share in her son's happiness, not his glory. She also wanted to catch up with friends and family, and they all knew who she was.

Other elders were there in spirit – those from the area who had gone before, represented by rows of framed photographs of the fallen displayed outside the wharenui (meeting house), and accompanied by kuia (female elders) who took turns to make sure they were not left alone. Big video screens were in place to convey the action to the farthest reaches of the crowd.

The *Opotiki News* printed the day's itinerary, which scarcely conveyed the emotion of the occasion but showed that a) the media would be kept in their place and b) Saturday lunch had been scheduled at a sensible time given the amount of oratory that was likely to precede it:

Friday

10 a.m.   Media gathering re protocols, rules and regulations

Noon   Powhiri for Ngati Porou and their VC recipient Ngarimu

4 p.m.   Powhiri for Nga Puhi (Apiata's biological whanau)
       Throughout the day there will be items by Whanau-a-Apanui
       children and Army

Saturday

8.30 a.m.   Media gathering

9 a.m.   Powhiri for Te Arawa members from the Manahi whanau
       and Mataatua iwi

11 a.m.   Willie Apiata and VIPs' speeches, Helen Clark, Chief of
       Defence, etc.

1 p.m.   Laying of a wreath in front of marae

2 p.m.   Informal media press conference

3 p.m.   Lunch and poro poro aki [farewell speeches]

Friday was a low-key affair, with Willie in civvies and not much in the way of formalities. When it was over, he had told Sam he would take him to stay the night under the stars at his other turangawaewae, The Land. Willie had slept there on Thursday night, a vigil of solitude before the intensity of the homecoming. When he saw them earlier in the day the Army Sergeant Major had asked Willie where he was spending the night.

'We're staying up the road,' said Willie.

'Where up the road – your aunty's place?' asked the Sergeant Major.

'No, in the bush.'

'Rubbish.'

Willie had had enough by about 3 a.m. and he and Sam left. As they drove up the road, the Sergeant Major followed them. The pair reached The Land, lit a fire and settled down with a bottle of wine and started to unwind properly over a quiet drink. Willie had got changed. His clothes and his Victoria Cross for New Zealand were hung from the branch of a tree. The Sergeant Major still took some convincing that this was where the nation's hero and one of the most senior and respected members of the SAS were going to be spending the night.

Saturday was the main event and Corporal Willie Apiata, VC, was in uniform. Conches blew to signal the start of the ceremony. Willie walked on, his medals on his chest, and accepted the challenge by picking up a wooden patu (club) from Te Kaha. He was then draped in a magnificent korowai (cloak).

Oratory followed, speaker after speaker praising Willie's achievement. At their conclusion he was presented with a taonga (treasure) of great worth, a pounamu mere (greenstone club). A haka to do credit to the god of earthquakes, Ruaumoko, followed. There could not have been a more appropriate deity to invoke on this auspicious occasion. Then Willie greeted the veterans who were present. He recalls his impressions of his reception:

Te Kaha felt like home. I went there because I had spent so much of my life there. It was out of respect for those people. They are good people, too, and people still talk about that weekend now.

I class Te Whanau-a-Apanui and Ngati Porou as my home because I was seven when I left the north. My whanau came down after my parents split up and these people accepted us – not just the Parkinsons, but the whole of the whanau.

You don't get accepted by just one person when you move into a place like that. Mum is a Pakeha, and the only things that make us Maori are our name and the blood that runs through the kids. There is a bit of a trial – like a selection course – that goes on when you move into an area and you have to prove yourself. The old lady is a hard old girl, and she had no worries in proving herself. People accepted her and they looked after us.

But on the day, it was an awesome event. I had been on that marae many times, but this was an experience I'll carry with me for the rest of my life. When I spoke, I spoke with the feeling I was getting off the people there. And I found it exhausting, because every time somebody touches me, they take a bit of energy out of me. Those old marae are sacred, and as soon as you set foot on one you feel the spiritual energy from the ancestors and all the people past and present.

I don't have a lot of te reo [Maori language]. I know how to pronounce it properly and I have a few words, but I'm not fluent. However, sitting there that day and listening to those men speaking, you start to understand what they are saying just by hearing it.

They began by saying they wanted me to be a captain, and by the end of the speeches they said I needed to be promoted to general. They talked a lot about how good this was for Maori.

I spoke later at the lunch. I told the people that I was wearing the Victoria Cross for all the people serving in the forces and for all the people there and for New Zealand.

I have a friend here in the SAS who is a spiritual man, and before I went I had asked him to write me a small speech in Maori so I could stick to the protocol for a place like that. I wanted to respect the Maoridom that surrounds that area and not offend anyone. But I only took out of what he wrote for me what I thought was applicable, because I knew that both peoples wanted to hear something – not just Maori. And it came out how I felt they wanted to hear it. I think you can prepare for these things too much. The best thing is to feel what everyone's feeling, and then what you want to say will come to you.

Everything I said came from my heart. I don't rehearse a speech or write anything down. I like to absorb the atmosphere, feel what people are feeling, listen to what they are saying, because then you can reply in a manner that you know they will be able to appreciate.

A lot of what Maori say in speeches are poems, and I finished with a small poem that went: 'Pull out the centre of the flax bush and where will the bellbird rest?' Meaning, I say, what is the most important thing in life? It's the people. That poem means a lot to me, and I wanted to let everybody there know what was important to me.

A lot of fence mending was happening that day – the history between Nga Puhi and Ngati Porou at Te Kaha is quite ferocious. Way back, Nga Puhi went down there and basically slaughtered their way to East Cape, because they had muskets, then went back home again. It wasn't until later, when they got muskets of their own, that the tribe retaliated. Last time Nga Puhi travelled down was for war, but now they came for peace.

This was the first time that those two tribes had stood on one marae in about 100 years. And when they referred to the history on that day, they did it in a jovial way. There was nothing vindictive about it. So I guess it's good that what happened to me has had such a positive effect.

At Te Kaha, Nga Puhi kaumatua (elder) and 28 (Maori) Battalion member Tamati Paraone asked Te Whanau-a-Apanui to bring Willie home to the north. He died before it happened, but his wish would be carried out.

Anyone who spends any amount of time with Willie knows that for all he is a man of action, he is also a thoughtful person who processes things with his heart as well as his head. He may be a reluctant speaker, but when he expresses himself it is with colour and passion. His could be called the philosophy of the hunter, because when you are in the bush on your own, or in a hootchie in a jungle trying not to make any noise, you get to spend a lot of time with your own thoughts. The homecoming at Te Kaha demonstrated Willie's close connection with his Maori heritage and Maori spirituality.

When his grandfather, Jim, died in 2000, he'd been living at Pukehina, a thin strip of Bay of Plenty beach. Jim was Pakeha, but as his coffin was being taken from the house for the funeral, and to everyone's surprise, Willie began an impromptu haka in homage to the old warrior. Two others present stepped forward to participate, but one look at Willie and they stopped in their tracks. They could see this was not their tribute to join.

Neighbours were drawn out of their houses by the commotion. Pukehina was a quiet place and this was a loud haka. All were gripped by an eerie stillness. As the hearse drove away, so the haka came to an end. Only then was the spell broken.

As with his oratory on the marae, Willie hadn't planned it, but he had known it was the right thing to do when it happened.

It's pretty intense how the old Maori people – and the young ones now – know so much about family. Anything you need to know about your family will be in somebody's head somewhere. And they will pass it down. We learn only a bit at school about some of the history of the ancestors.

I'm not a religious person, but I am spiritual within myself and in my family. Maori have our gods: the god of war, the god of the forest, Papatuanuku and

Ranginui – Sky and Earth. I was talking to one of the old badged members at work who knew about it. He explained that the god of war might not be an actual war god who was a spirit, but was more an idea that grew from someone who was a really aggressive person. He is the pinnacle of what a warrior can be. And the god of the forest was a man of the bush. And from those eras people remember the man of the sea and the man of the bush. That explained a lot to me.

I have a lot of respect for the bush and the ocean. Always, before I hop into the sea, I flick a bit of water on myself, and I wash my face before I go for a dive. When I walk into the bush, as I go across the first crossing, the first thing I do is chuck a bit of water over me, and that's my way of paying my respect to the bush, because I'm going up there to get a kai. If I come away with nothing I'm thankful to the bush, because I've still had a good experience.

One thing I'm really respectful of, and I like other people to respect, is my hands. These are what I make my living off, because I'm a practical person. I use my hands for everything. They are what make me. They help me get my kai, they dress up the meat that I have killed, they work the weapons that we use, they build everything that we make, they drive the car.

A welcome change of pace after the rituals and ceremonies of the previous few weeks came with Willie's participation in the re-enactment of the Afghan contact for the *Reluctant Hero* documentary.

He was invited to play himself but turned down the offer, opting instead to stay on the sidelines and help out as one of the gunners on another vehicle. It was wet and messy and hard work. He loved it. For realism, and because the SAS preferred it that way, live rounds were used in the shooting. To this day, many believe the footage seen in the documentary is of the actual event itself, as though the SAS has film crews accompanying it on its operations.

It was a brief return to almost-normality for Willie, who now seemed to be working for the Victoria Cross rather than the SAS. Similarly, his Commanding Officer, charged with overseeing so many of his arrangements in the managerial role, would tell Willie he felt like the highest-ranked PA in the Army at times. The VC was easily as demanding a master as the SAS.

Within days, Willie would be heading to London to meet the people behind the Victoria Cross and George Cross Association and pay a visit to the Commonwealth war cemetery at Passchendaele.

CHAPTER NINETEEN

EUROPE

Last time Willie went overseas he had flown in a roaring Hercules with all the discomfort that involves. When he travelled to London in September 2007, for 10 packed days of official Victoria Cross and New Zealand Defence Force duties there and in Belgium, he and Sam achieved that most elusive of goals – a very kind upgrade to business class courtesy of Air New Zealand. Willie still felt most at home sleeping under the stars or a hootchie, but he was learning to tolerate the privileges that come with recognition. In particular, he did a thorough job of working his way through the choices on the business-class menu between New Zealand and the UK.

The focus of this trip was ceremonies to mark the 90th anniversary of the Battle of Passchendaele, but he was also going to be spending time tending to his medal, which had its own needs. But first, he and Sam had a day to themselves and Willie wisely chose not to spend it sightseeing or visiting legendary pubs but relaxing in his hotel room, watching rugby on TV.

His first official duty was to lay a wreath at the grave of Lord Freyberg, former Governor-General of New Zealand and, more relevantly, a fellow VC holder. Freyberg's grave at St Martha's on the Hill Church had recently been restored after being allowed to fall into disrepair. Freyberg family members, several other New Zealand Defence Force personnel and the Prime Minister of New Zealand, a by now familiar figure to Willie, were there. Having laid his wreath he stood up, stepped back and saluted.

'That was the most tedious salute I've ever seen,' Sam told him later.

Willie was not going to argue. If proficiency in certain basics had been a pre-requisite for getting a VC, he would still be waiting for his.

I hate drill. I'm no good at marching and I can't salute to this day. When I was down in Waiouru on my road trip after I got my VC people would salute me and I would just give them a wave. I'm not an officer. I've been growled at so often in the past for walking past an officer and forgetting to salute, and before I know it he'd be yelling: 'Oi! Have you forgotten to do something?'

When I did my Junior NCO course, learning to be an instructor, we had to do drills. I had to do saluting on the march, and there was no way I could get it. I was already in the SAS, but when we do promotional courses we go back to the Regular Army to do them. You have to pull your hand up on a certain step, co-ordinate it with when your foot hits the ground, then walk another couple of steps and bring your hand down again, and you've got to carry on marching the whole time. You have your hand up for a certain number of paces, then down again for the same number. Nine times out of 10, when I put my arm down to carry on marching, I would go into a goon march – when your arm swings in the same time as your leg on both sides. Once you start goon marching, you can't get out of it. You have to stop, walk for a bit and then get back into step, and at the end of it, you're getting abuse from everyone.

And I hated standing in one spot for ages. It takes a lot of discipline to do it. When you do finally start marching, it's better, but I'm a bit deaf and I always half hear a move. The worst thing you can do is move half a second after everyone else. All that people watching notice is the one who's out of place.

His award had brought with it eligibility for membership of the Victoria Cross and George Cross Association: patron, the Queen; president, the Prince of Wales. It was founded in 1956 so that members could meet each other regularly. Obviously, there were a lot more than the current 13 VC holders then.

One of the first letters Willie received congratulating him on his award was from the association's chairman, Jim Beaton, a former royal bodyguard who was awarded the George Cross for protecting Princess Anne during a 1974 kidnap attempt in which he was shot. A major aim of the association is to enable members to help each other. It has a benevolent fund to assist any who are in dire need, established because, as Beaton wrote in his letter, there were many sad stories of VC holders 'dying penniless and forgotten' in years gone by.

Although Willie was a long way from meeting either of those fates, there were other obvious advantages to being in touch with fellow VC winners. One was the opportunity to attend the biennial reunions, albeit, as Beaton wrote, 'our gatherings are not enormous'. The association was run by people, he said, who had been through what

Willie had been through 'and care to mind their own business'. And that was what held most appeal for Willie – he would be able to talk to people who understood what he had experienced. Furthermore, they would be people who, in most cases, were considerably older than himself and might have something to teach him.

An observation by the secretary of the association, Mrs Didy Grahame, describing its members, also seemed to suggest Willie would find himself among kindred spirits. 'They are like a family,' she told him. 'Courage is a given, but they are very humble people. They admire each other, but they think of themselves as unworthy.'

Willie Apiata to a T.

Grahame has a saying that is also relevant to the experience of all VC holders and lies behind the association's aims, particularly for its newer members: 'It is important to protect the innocent from the unscrupulous until such time as they can determine the difference.'

Just as his Commanding Officer looked after Willie's affairs with a focus on the SAS, the association looked after his interests as they related to the VC. Although he would not meet any fellow holders on this trip – that would not happen until the scheduled reunion in September 2008 – Willie got to know Beaton and Grahame and warmed quickly to both.

Her efforts on his behalf went beyond the merely formal. At the Freyberg ceremony, a Scottish businessman had offered to send Willie and Sam to the All Blacks' World Cup game in Paris. Willie explained that was the day they were due to return home, and they were obliged to stick to their schedule. Didy Grahame offered to take the matter up with Helen Clark, who happened to be walking past at the time.

'Willie's his own man, he can go to the game if he wants to,' responded the PM.

Grahame then put it to the New Zealand Brigadier who was present. He referred it to the CO who was considerably less enthusiastic. Plan A was adhered to.

Willie also met General Sir Peter de la Billiere, Commander-in-Chief of British Forces in the 1990 Gulf War and, closer to Willie's heart, an SAS member who was involved in many of its most famous operations. He was director of the service during the Iranian embassy siege of 1980. Many people first heard of the SAS during this operation, when members of the Regiment stormed the building and rescued the hostages.

They had lunch together before an appointment at Defence House. Willie had taken with him a patu which the New Zealand SAS had arranged as a gift for Sir Peter. He introduced Willie to the concept of the three noes, which he said Willie would find very useful in years to come: 'No, not today. No, not tomorrow. No, not ever.'

After one bottle of wine, Sir Peter, who is retired, said: 'Do you feel like another bottle, Willie?'

'As long as you're going to help me, I don't mind giving you a hand,' was the reply.

Willie's grin was wider than usual, and his cheeks positively rosy by the time he got to the more formal part of the afternoon's activities at Defence House. The centre holds a Victoria Cross and George Cross Memorial that Didy Grahame had arranged and was keen for Willie to see – a sculpture showing the figure of a soldier emerging from a rock.

Willie admired the sculpture in its impressive surroundings, and was spellbound to see the register of Victoria Crosses that has been kept since the very first was awarded a century and a half ago. The register is up to its second volume, and Willie's is the last name entered. Turning the leaves slowly, he gazed at the pages of history, paying most attention to the names from his own country, including those from the New Zealand Wars.

Another memorable encounter on this visit was with Patrick Nolands, an expatriate who is the only New Zealander working as a beefeater at the Tower of London, where Willie met him on a visit with Grahame. Several months afterwards, Nolands wrote to Willie enclosing a group of medals from his collection. It included a miniature Victoria Cross, made by Hancocks themselves, that had been given to a Victorian officer. Nolands gave this valuable set to Willie simply because Willie's award had made him 'proud to be a New Zealander'. Those miniatures now rest with Willie's own medal in their glass case at Rennie Lines.

Jim Beaton offered to take him to Buckingham Palace and asked him what he wanted to see. Willie was only interested in the horses, so a tour of the stables was arranged. He marvelled at the ornate, heavy and opulent carriages as Beaton explained who used which ones and on what occasions.

He also met the Director of Special Forces, which includes 22 SAS, who gave him a treasured picture representing the history of the 22nd Special Air Service.

'Do you ride?' the DSF asked me.

'Do I ride what, sir?'

'Do you ride a horse?'

'Oh yeah, I ride horses.'

'Would you like to come for a ride?'

He asked if I had riding boots and britches and I said, 'No, I've got my track pants and sneakers.' I turned up in those, but before you knew it they had rustled up a pair of britches and these riding boots that come all the way up to your knee. Sam had been invited to come on the ride and wasn't sure if he would or not. When he saw the outfit, he said, no thanks.

There was no putting your foot in the stirrup and throwing your leg over. They led the horse – mine was called Kosovo – up to a set of concrete steps and you walked up them and climbed on. Then we went for a ride around Hyde Park.

'You've got to watch out for this bugger,' said the soldier whose horse it was. 'He's a bit flighty; he's got quite a bit of spirit in him.'

I've got hunting horses at home with more spirit, but it's because their horses are huge so they can carry all that armour and handle the weight of the carriages. They're like a cross between a quarter horse and a draught horse. And they're quiet too, because they are in town where there are lots of crowds, and they are trained to stay calm.

While in London, Willie also spent a riotous night with three former Commanding Officers of 1 NZSAS GP that was arranged by his CO, one of whom had been in command on his first tour of Afghanistan. Another night, he was entertained by local 22 SAS boys and introduced to the delights of riding on the Tube, steak and kidney pie and, less enthusiastically, warm Guinness. He was reminded how the brotherhood that is formed in the shared experiences of selection and cycle can last over the years and across the globe.

In Belgium, Willie was due to attend a wreath-laying ceremony at the Messines Ridge New Zealand Memorial, an Anzac service, and a service of reinterment for five Australian soldiers whose remains had been found. The focus was the Passchendaele anniversary. One of the most disastrous battles of the First World War, Passchendaele saw five miles of ground gained for some 140,000 lives lost. On 12 October 1917, 845 New Zealanders were either killed or fatally wounded. More New Zealanders lost their lives in battle on that day than on any other day in any other war. By the time the fighting was over, 3596 New Zealanders were dead. Of those, 519 are buried at nearby Tyne Cot Commonwealth War Graves Cemetery, which holds a total of nearly 12,000 graves.

This trip saw a large number of New Zealanders in Belgium for the occasion, including the Prime Minister, the Chief of Defence Force and numerous other notables based in Europe. Willie was also moved to see a large number of returned servicemen, who had made the journey from the other side of the world.

But there were agendas at work which were not always in line with what Willie would want for such a pilgrimage. Everyone seemed to need a piece of the VC winner and he tried hard to give as much of himself as he could. But it seemed at times like he could never give enough. Fortunately, Sam would be there to protect him if things started to get out of control.

The CO's master plan was for me to be exposed to the history of where a lot of VCs were won. He was right. To go to a battleground on an actual field where a huge amount of life was lost is shocking.

The people there remember those who fell every single evening with a service. At Tyne Cot the walls are covered in thousands of names, and there are so many warriors who are only 'known to God'. It's a stunning place.

The Germans' pillboxes are still there. They were fighting from their fortified position and we were fighting in the mud. They built up and we dug down. That's why the Germans had a much better, superior fighting position than us. They also had machine gunning down to an absolute art, and they sat in the pillboxes and kept firing.

Before the battle the area had been bombed and the dykes burst. The place was flooded and turned into a swamp. The roads disappeared. And then it was raining constantly. If you weren't killed by an artillery shell or a bullet, you drowned in the mud. The men who fell knew they were going to die when they walked out of their trenches. Not one of them came back. It's unreal, the commitment they had to take that step out of the trench.

The Kiwis were only allowed to walk. They weren't allowed to run or take cover the way we do when we fight now. By the time they began to move, the Germans had set up all their guns in all their positions and started mowing us down. A lot of guys were getting stuck in the mud. When you comprehend the sacrifice they made – you feel so unworthy.

It's a very quiet and solemn place. On the morning we were there, it was covered in mist, and you couldn't even hear a bird chirping. But you could feel the presence of the warriors.

At Tyne Cot there is a memorial listing the names of the fallen, many of whose bodies were never found. In fact, bodies still come to light today, which is why the Australian soldiers were being reburied.

It is one thing to see the rows of headstones in a still or moving image. It is another altogether to stand in the middle of them and realise that each one represents a young life lost. Sam came across the list of names of New Zealanders who had been killed but never found. A stunned Willie had begun to get quite emotional when a TV journalist tried to ask him how it made him feel.

Willie had received an assurance before he left that, even though there would be media at Passchendaele, he would not be expected to do any interviews. However he felt, he did not feel like talking. A defence media adviser tried to persuade him to give an interview. He was doing his job, but he wasn't doing what Willie wanted.

This was where the mentor came into his own, because he had

known some of the people in senior positions – which also meant, now, senior to him – when they were starting out. He had been tasked by the CO to ensure Willie's welfare and that was what he was going to do. He was close enough to Willie to read the signs that he needed a break. And if the pressure and people were getting too much, one look from the VC hero would see Sam move in and extract him.

Willie's politeness continued to be sorely tried. But he could hardly have been clearer.

'I'm not over here to talk to the TV,' he said. 'It's not what I'm going to do and the answer is no, I'm not going to do it today, tomorrow or the next day, so quit asking me.'

Eventually, he had a word to a member of the Prime Minister's staff over lunch. They promised to take care of it, and that was the end of that.

Willie felt as though he hadn't been able to make the most of his time at Tyne Cot. So he and Sam broke ranks. Sam told the relevant superior he and Willie were deviating from the official programme, at a time when the superior was due to be accompanying the Prime Minister. He and Willie went back alone to the cemetery, although Willie did stop to tell the *Reluctant Hero* crew where he would be. They were welcome to tag along – and by 'along' he meant a long way from him. They kept their distance.

The pair decided to try to touch every New Zealand headstone at the cemetery. As the sun set they moved through the rows of white, saying tena koe to each of their countrymen as they found them. It was dark by the time they left.

Willie took with him a new understanding of what sacrifice meant. He had understood it before, now he could feel it in his heart.

CHAPTER TWENTY

PAPAKURA

Back at Rennie Lines, the Victoria Cross continued to bring with it an astonishing number of commitments, requests and obligations that had to be dealt with. To meet its special requirements, Willie got his own office – a small cubicle not far from the eye of his Commanding Officer – and a BlackBerry (which is not to be confused with the 'bro phone' he reserves for his intimates). The office has a framed copy of the Hubbard cartoon of Willie and the Black Power gang members, and also contains the 'Willie VC' archive. He has kept all his mail so his son will one day be able to read it and understand what his father's award has meant to so many people.

He lives by his Outlook appointment calendar. Most mornings, between PT and his real work, he spends some time with his computer. He likes to oblige by responding favourably to autograph requests, although he is wary of pleas for multiple copies that look like the writer might be planning to sell them on. In the wake of the award, he has received congratulatory mail from, among many others, the Long Range Desert Group Association – survivors of the band who played a part in the formation of the first SAS; what feels like every Returned Services Association in the country; individual former SAS members, including the unit's Colonel Commandant; the 28th Maori Battalion Association; Prince Charles (from whom, plus Camilla, Willie now also gets a Christmas card); and the Ex-Vietnam Services Association.

With his general respect for older and wiser heads, Willie has a special place in his heart for the RSA. He finds it strange that his official photo is on the wall of RSAs, because to his mind, for your photo to be on an RSA wall, you have to be dead. Willie doesn't particularly like being photographed, and he dislikes seeing his photo in newspapers or magazines. Personally, he would rather not be on those RSA walls, but he knows that for those keeping military tradition alive in New Zealand he is important. The awkwardness he feels is outweighed by the amount of inspiration and joy his deeds have brought to others. And that means he belongs on their walls. Also, such is his respect for returned servicemen that there is little he wouldn't do for them.

We went down to Palmerston North for a wedding. It was a couple of hours before we needed to be there. We all had our suits on and went into the RSA across the road from the church. That was fun, because I had no moustache and no one recognised me. I had shaved it off for diving because I can't wear a mask properly if I have my moustache.

So no one twigged. I grabbed the boys some handles but the boys were disappointed.

'No free beers?'

'No, bro. Incognito.'

It was a good feeling. I was able to let my hair down a little bit and I even went nightclubbing and stayed out late.

I have to be on my toes all the time now. I used to go out with my mates a lot and let rip. I was my old jovial self with not a care in the world.

If I do go out with the boys, people still come up and want to say hello and get photos of me, and it's not fair on the lads. We like to keep to ourselves, and me being with them draws attention to my mates as well.

One of the most meaningful tributes Willie has been paid is the award by the RSA of the Badge in Gold, its rarely granted highest honour. Willie received it on Armistice Day 2007, as did, post-humously, 21 other New Zealand VC recipients.

He might have the medal, but Willie Apiata feels no braver nor more of a soldier than these veterans, and to be so honoured by them was humbling. He is conscious that they fought in wars of no fixed duration. They didn't go for three-month or six-month tours – they went and stayed away until the job was done. They didn't have the technology of the modern soldier, but they had incred-ible courage and commitment. In a relatively short time, they saw more action than a soldier like Willie is likely to see in his entire career.

I've been lucky. I've met a lot of people in my life and watched how they work. You see them oozing with experience. Old people have shared many things with me. They might be small things, but those small things have helped a lot in the long run.

We are just carriers of information, and it's our job to pass it on to the next generation. I would like to be able to help the generation coming up – not necessarily wayward kids, but kids who have some sort of direction. People helped me a lot, so I would like to give back to them and eventually to people in wider New Zealand.

But I wouldn't be telling them what to do. That's not up to me. Every man makes his own choices. You either take this road or that road. Some dudes prefer to be professional at breaking the law. They become proficient at that, and it's not until they get caught that their actions catch up with them. When you're growing up and make a mistake, you always learn from it.

My aim, before they start shovelling the soil on me, is to hand over what I've been taught to the young people, because it wasn't mine. It was given to me from the people I grew up with, and they didn't keep it to themselves. I love instructing. That's the position I'm in with the SAS now.

I want to go home and have young fellas come down and break in a few horses. The young ones who are there know how to hunt. They know how to get a kai. Those skills are still there. They've got all the potential but the thing missing is – have these buggers got any goals? They haven't journeyed out to make their mark in life, or they've become content with the situation. They're not really happy. They're just content with going on day to day.

The main thing I tell kids when I talk to them is to respect their parents and others and live every day to the fullest. And always have a goal, because if you don't, then you've got nothing to strive for. The first goal you choose may not be the right one for you, but you will find that out along your journey through life. It evolves until you find that thing you really, really want to do and then you will go for it.

Whoever stole 102 medals from the Waiouru Military Museum in December 2007, they clearly hadn't thought through the goal they had chosen for themselves. The medals, which included Charles Upham's VC with its bar, were impossible to sell. They weren't even worth melting down. This was a theft from the nation, and people felt violated in the same way individuals do when their homes have been burgled. New Zealanders were appalled by the act. And they soon got to know the name of Lord Michael Ashcroft.

The world's most assiduous private collector of Victoria Crosses, Ashcroft is chairman of BB Holdings, which has interests in several areas, including finance and telecommunications, and is deputy chairman of the British Conservative Party. He has assembled a collection of 142 VCs which officially belong to a trust set up to care for them. He is also the author of *Victoria Cross Heroes*, and he offered a reward of $200,000 for the safe return of the stolen Waiouru medals.

Before that money was paid out, however, other methods would be tried to get the medals back. Willie made his first community service advertisement, pleading for their return. At the head of a line-up of TV stars and sports heroes, he did his duty. 'We don't want to know why you did it – we just want the medals back,' he told the camera. His performance lacked for nothing next to those of the more seasoned celebrities he appeared alongside. No one watching would have guessed he had been pulled out of a lecture minutes before, shoved in front of a camera, and told to say the words before being sent back again. His mind had really been elsewhere, but it was like all Willie's public appearances: the exterior was rock solid, no matter what was going on inside.

Not that it made any difference. The pleas went unheeded. The medals were eventually returned and the reward paid. In the meantime, Lord Ashcroft had visited New Zealand where, naturally, he wanted to meet the world's newest VC holder. To the businessman's delight, Willie took the down-to-earth peer shooting on the range at the unit's Battle Training Facility. And Ashcroft endeared himself to Willie in turn by spending much of his time winding up the SAS's Commanding Officer, who delighted in it and gave as good as he got.

'When you come to the UK,' Ashcroft told the CO on leaving, 'I'd like to have you to the House of Lords for a decent cup of tea. Let me know when you are coming and I will send you a book on etiquette, because you are certainly lacking in it.' Lord Ashcroft got the last laugh and his visit was a highlight.

Photos were taken of the three men in various combinations. Ashcroft said he would keep the one of himself with Willie.

Naturally, Willie was keen to learn what he could from one of the world's foremost experts on the Victoria Cross, but their time together was all too brief. By now, Willie knew all about having to keep to a schedule. He also appreciated that Ashcroft knew better than to ask him the dreaded 'So, what exactly happened in Afghanistan?' question.

Ashcroft was just one of many visitors to Rennie Lines these days wanting to 'meet the VC'. Willie is usually happy to meet them because, if they have SAS business, they are likely to be people with something of interest about them. In the middle of 2008 several US Vietnam veterans were guests. As others had before them, they warned Willie of the dangers that came with the sort of award he had received. They had former comrades whose Medals of Honour, the US bravery award closest to the Victoria Cross, had been more a curse than a blessing as they succumbed to the free drinks, hero worship, and a life that was all looking back at past glories and no looking ahead to the future.

Today, when the Commanding Officer hosts people to lunch in

the mess, he is used to seeing their eyes wander around the room until they settle on Willie and stay there, fascinated. Call it a hunter's instinct, but one of the few things that makes Willie uncomfortable is being stared at. He is approached and greeted wherever he goes, and is happy to shake a hand and say hello. But simply being stared at, he finds unsettling.

Willie has had to train himself to deal with all the attention and expectations. He has had help from his unit, particularly in fending off people for whom his image and the qualities others associate with him would be powerful commercial tools. The Army itself is holding back from maximising Willie's potential. There will be no posters of Willie Apiata pointing and saying HE WANTS YOU FOR THE NZ ARMY put up on recruiting office walls around the country.

Numerous invitations are received from people who want to confer other awards on him. He has even been invited to present an award to a brave dog. He has been offered, and accepted, life membership of the Australian Returned Services League. Obviously these various offers require differing responses. Many invitations go first to Defence Headquarters where they are turned down flat because they would contravene policy. Others are filtered through the Commanding Officer. Willie carries his boss's business card with him, so that he can give it to people and they can request his presence formally in writing so that it can be considered fairly with all the others. Willie's first instinct is to say yes to any request. Fortunately for him, his boss's first instinct is to say no. It is easy to forget that he is still a member of an elite branch of the armed forces with a job that has responsibilities and certain constraints that come with that. Simply put, he is still required to work for his living. If he is away too much then he will be unable to progress with his professional competencies.

It will be a long time before Willie will be capable of or enthusiastic about speaking for an hour to a room full of people in evening dress. In the meantime, he's used to getting the same questions over and over: 'How are you coping? Are they leaving you alone yet?' Well, perhaps if people stopped coming up to him and asking him if they were leaving him alone yet, he might get a bit of peace. But he is always happy to give time to veterans and children.

He is not a reader, except when on operations and there is a lot of downtime, but everyone gives him books with military themes. Any spare time he does have will be spent in the bush, not curled up on the couch with a good book. At least, on that far-off day when he can no longer get himself into the bush to go hunting, he will have plenty to read.

People have expectations not just of Willie as a VC winner but as a member of the SAS as well – their interest piqued by the dark and dangerous maverick side of the unit's reputation. He doesn't mind talking about the unit, but would rather chat to people about what they do for a living. After all, he already knows about the SAS.

At home it's different. People there are glad to see me, and I'm glad to have a beer with them. I can walk around in the clothes that I feel comfortable in, my hunting gears straight out of the bush, stinking of blood from carrying the animal out. They treat me like they used to before I had the VC, but there is still that thing there.

If I had my way I would disappear into the bush. I didn't want all the attention, but it comes with the award. There is no way you could give it back. You could go to the cells and die by the guillotine, but they can never take the award off you. It's the highest award you can get, but it's a burden at the same time. The hardest thing I find every day is trying to be me.

It follows me everywhere. Once we went on an Australian submarine at Devonport. Whenever they turn up we like to have a look around and see how things work – at least, the areas they're allowed to show us. We did a bit of diving around it too, so I didn't have my moustache either.

We gave them a bottle of SAS port to say thanks and had a yarn with them. I was just one of the boys, and it wasn't until we were about to leave that they realised who I was. Then things changed. As I was walking off they had a dude blowing a whistle and the officer of the day was standing on the top of the ramp, paying me a compliment as I walked off.

I was staggered. I didn't even call him 'Sir'. I just said, 'Cheers, man, thanks for that.' What do you do?

CHAPTER TWENTY-ONE

WAITANGI

When Willie gave his Victoria Cross and other medals to the unit, a few days before Anzac Day 2008, some thought he had been pressured into doing so. They saw the SAS making the most of a once-in-a-lifetime PR opportunity. But Willie isn't easy to pressure, and the idea of giving his VC to 'the boys' was hardly new. It had occurred to him around the time he got it. His CO, who predicted, accurately, that he would be charged with having talked Willie into the gesture, insisted he take his time thinking about it. Eventually Willie had to tell him to stop asking if he was sure this was what he wanted to do. He was sure.

From Willie's point of view it had several advantages. The terms of the gift, organised by the administrators of the trust that had been set up for him, meant he, and his son after him, have access to the medals whenever they want them. The Victoria Cross is like a talisman in a legend that has the power to do good or evil depending on the motives of the person holding it. But the terms also protect his boy or anyone else from the temptation of selling it. Most importantly, it was the right thing to do, because, in Willie's mind, the medal already belonged to the unit. This was just the paperwork.

The medal now resides in a small glass case in a corner of group headquarters. He also chose the accompanying photo. It isn't the official uniformed photograph that was taken for the announcement of his award, or a stiff military portrait. It is a picture of the real Willie, in Afghanistan, all but unrecognisable behind beard, sunglasses and shemagh.

If Willie had been given a choice, he would have accepted his VC not at Government House with speeches and a piano playing an anthem, but in the boss's office with a handshake and a quiet 'Good work, Willie'. Similarly, if he had had his way he might have handed it over in the team shed after a workout, as casually as possible, before heading up to the MOE house to blast the cobwebs away, or over to the Hunting Lodge for a beer. At this point, however, the CO drew a line. This was a piece of New Zealand history unfolding and it had at least to be recorded. The gift of the VC took place in front of the cameras and became the climax of the *Reluctant Hero* documentary.

However, Willie had to see and approve the documentary before it went to air, a task he found excruciating. Watching the re-enactment of the Afghanistan contact he found particularly hard. The CO sat where he could observe Willie watching himself, alert for any signs of major discomfort. None showed. As with other public appearances, in person or through the media, Willie would have preferred it not to have been made, but accepted that since it was going to be aired this was as good as he could expect.

'Boss, that's great,' he said. 'But I can never watch it again.'

And he never has, although his 14 nephews and nieces watch it repeatedly. He got copies to give the family but his sister bought one herself because she couldn't wait.

Soon after the documentary's well-received Anzac Day screening, Willie was off to Waitangi where he would be welcomed home and feted by his father's people. Following Tamati Paraone's request at Te Kaha, Nga Puhi had been keen for Willie to revisit his father's home marae at Oromahoe for many months before it happened. The occasion was, inevitably, similar to the Te Kaha homecoming.

As at the earlier event, he was celebrated by the people who had raised him. Now he would be paid tribute by those whose blood he shared, his father's people. The contact had lapsed for many years. And before seeing them he needed to see his father.

I needed to find him. They think he is in prison, but he's not. He's just living the old Maori way. He's got a few battle scars, and he is quite worn.

I needed him to understand what was happening to me.

I call him up from time to time and go and have a cup of tea with him.

It had been 21 years, but he will always be my father. I'm so glad I found him. It ended badly but he has stayed away from us and I take my hat off to him for that. He left us in peace and didn't try to push his way back into our lives. My sisters say, 'When we're ready, we'll go see the old man.' That's their choice.

When I went up to Waitangi, I found I was related to so many people in some fashion or other. My father came from a family of 16, so there were heaps of aunts and uncles for a start.

The people at Te Kaha I had known all my life. I had grown up with them, because I was brought up and raised there. My heart told me that was the first place I needed to go back to – to honour them for what they had done for me. Going back to the Nga Puhi at Waitangi was a lot different. Although it was where my bloodline was, I remembered very little of the place because I was very young when I left. I remembered my grandmother, Erana Apiata, and I knew a few of the old man's brothers.

Mum, Sam and I went to do a recce of the marae the day before, like we had done at Government House before the investiture, but when we got there we realised we didn't have the right to be there yet. So we turned the wagon around and went home.

I was very happy to be there. If you are from a tribe, there's always a little itch in there about where you're from. I brought my trustees up for it. I told them, 'If you want to experience Maori culture, this would be the time. You will get a real good education and get to know me and my family a bit better.'

I don't know how to explain the feeling that goes through you when you walk on, and you see not only all those people who are living, but you also feel the presence of the dead who have come to check it out as well. I said to my mate, 'It's going to rain as soon as we walk on to that marae.'

The sun was out when we turned up, but as soon as we gathered together to walk on to the marae and took the first step, the sky opened with rain – just for that one moment. And that was our ancestors weeping for me. I had come home and they had come to celebrate. It stayed like that until we got to the meeting house. I had to stop walking for a moment because the presence was so strong. I had had the same feeling in Te Kaha.

I walked on at Tukaki in Ta Kaha with Pita Apiata, the kaumatua of the Apiata family, and Tamati Paraone, from the 28th Maori Battalion Association, on my left and right – those are some very honourable men. To be awarded a VC and be standing next to those two, I felt unworthy. Those guys had seen more war than I will ever see in my lifetime. Tamati passed away prior to my return north, but Pita was still there. He spoke of his good friend and how much he missed him, which made me feel for the old fella.

As we were walking on, the warriors challenged me to make sure I came in good faith. They lay down the challenge and handed me a wooden spear that is in my room now. After that, one took off his headband and laid it down on the ground. Then all the other warriors proceeded to do the same. I've never seen that happen before. Once the last one was laid, I gathered them up. I wasn't expecting to speak when I did, but I found myself talking while one of the kaumatua was speaking. It started to come out of me and everything went totally quiet. All I could hear was the women weeping.

I began speaking in Maori because that's the way they are up there. The co-ordinator had said there would be no more talking in English, but I am Maori and Pakeha, so I opened my speech in Maori, saying, 'The birds are calling and now I am calling to the people.' And then I thanked the Lord and told them what I was feeling. How I was raised in the lands of Ngati Porou, and Te Whanau-a-Apanui, and I was sent down from Nga Puhi when I was a little fella and other people brought me up. And how, when I was of age, I journeyed out into the world to find my calling. And how I have finally come home a warrior, and a soldier, and a humble person. I said we were all united as proud Maori, as proud people, proud New Zealanders, that we were all one. And I repeated that poem from Te Kaha. To finish with, I said the most important thing in life will always be the people because without them you are nothing.

After my speech all the military, Maori and Pakeha, who had come up to help with food and transport did a haka. That's the military way – whatever our culture or race, our uniform makes us one.

I was also happy to see some of the old fellas there who had been at Passchendaele. I remembered their faces and was able to have a word with them.

Overall, it was exhausting. There were all sorts of people wanting me to do all sorts of things. The boss always sends an officer with me, someone who can step in and say, 'Hey, no, this is what's happening and this is why he's coming with us.' I felt sorry for the people, because they really wanted me to stay on, but because of the programme and the way things were organised, it was impossible.

But I did thank the cooks. That's how I was brought up. You like to meet the people who dug the hangi and peeled the spuds and washed the dishes. They're the ones who have driven the whole event, because if there's no kai, people get grumpy. Even at home, if you've had a feed you always cruise up and thank your wife or your mum.

At Waitangi Willie received more gifts to add to those he had been given since his award was announced. He has been the recipient of some extraordinary taonga in those months. Many connect him with his ancestors and traditions. And a number are on display in the trophy room at Rennie Lines where Willie's mementoes have a shelf to themselves.

At Te Kaha there were the wooden patu and pounamu mere. He received two whalebone taonga – one from his Parkinson whanau, made of bone more than a century old. There were mere at Waitangi too, and a marvellous tokotoko or whakapapa stick depicting his genealogy, so that he will always know where he comes from.

He is as gracious in the receipt of such gifts as he is in thanking the cooks or others who have helped him, always with the naturally correct response for any situation. One observer at Waitangi noted how when he was given a taonga he held his hand over both the gift and the hand of the giver for a long time, as though drawing a little of their spirit into it. Willie knew that beyond their intrinsic value, these offerings represent both the time taken to make them and more intangible qualities of respect and connection.

When you pick something up, it either feels good in your hand, or it doesn't. You feel it when you pick it up, you can tell as soon as you put the cord around your hand and grasp it that it's travelling through centuries.

The taonga I wear round my neck is stone. It's heavy but it's warm all the time. I was given that at Waitangi and I haven't taken it off since. I had a greenstone cross that Charles Upham's driver, John Hurren, gave me. My son wears that.

The patu is from whalebone that's over a hundred years old and came up from the Marlborough Sounds. It feels moist, whereas the one from up north feels like it's made of stone.

I want to find out all the stories of these taonga so that when it comes time to hand them over to my son, he knows exactly what each one means: who gave them to me and where they came from; who had them before me.

Everything Willie has been given has been an attempt by the giver to express what he and his honour mean to them, and how much they respect his achievement. For Willie and for those closest to him, however, the best thing about the accolade is not that he got it, but how it has made other people feel. His mother, who has had her share of congratulations as she has accompanied her son around the country, probably puts it best.

'It means people coming together finally instead of being apart,' says his mum. 'I saw that when we went to Waitangi. Aren't there people ready to crush that Waitangi Treaty? I don't think they're going to do that now, after what happened when we were up there. When I look around and I see the kids and I see tears, I see people that have got a reason to carry on and fight for New Zealand – not for the whole world, just for our nation, for our beliefs and our rights. It can be done. One person has just proved it. See, it can be done.'

Willie Apiata's future comes in two parts: the short term and the long term. The short-term future would be getting back to work. As he and his Commanding Officer have to keep reminding people, he has a day job. He is a member of the SAS.

It is widely, if bizarrely, believed that Willie is now too 'valuable' to be allowed to return to operational duty where his life could be put at risk again. Which is to suggest that everybody else in the unit is expendable. It is also to say that his profile and mana as New Zealand's most highly decorated living soldier mean he has to be protected like a delicate piece of porcelain. But he and his boss don't see it that way. It would be paradoxical indeed to give someone an award for bravery and then tell him he won't be given an opportunity to display that bravery again.

One of Willie's earliest requests when he was given his VC was to be allowed to continue working normally and do the job he signed up to do. He was promised that he would. Things aren't quite back to normal yet, but the day will come. The only activities that may be ruled out for him are highly discreet tasks such as close protection work, where his recognisability could draw attention and do more to endanger than safeguard the person under protection. On other operations, especially overseas, that wouldn't be a problem. For the rest of the time, behind a gas mask or balaclava, he is just another man in a uniform.

He worries that with the demands the VC makes on his time he is falling behind with training that his colleagues are undertaking, and that those who started after him may end up getting ahead. But both they and he know that he will work to catch up as he did before when, for instance, he caught up on pepper spraying. The commitment and drive Willie displayed when he trained for selection are still strong.

He turned down a promotion before his award. Having just returned to the SAS from his months away helping at the Officer Cadet School at Waiouru, he felt he needed to prove himself and earn back the respect of his fellow Group members after his absence. He doesn't like to receive anything unless he is convinced he's earned it. While he has ambitions within the SAS, they do not go as far as might be expected of someone with his status. The regimental sergeant major's role would allow him to mentor young people and pass on valuable knowledge, and that is the limit of his ambition at this stage.

RSM is several steps up the ladder for band four qualified Corporal Willie Apiata – corporal to sergeant, staff sergeant, sergeant major, and warrant officer class one, which is regimental sergeant major. In the modern Army a soldier has to meet strict criteria for promotion. You cannot jump ranks. Spontaneous advancement based on the cut of someone's jib or, say, some spectacular feat of bravery, just doesn't happen. VC or no VC, Willie Apiata has to do courses, gain qualifications and experience, and endure a stand-down period between levels before he can aim for promotion. Just like any other soldier. He has to be trained to a certain level of competence and demonstrate that competence – a man promoted before he has all the skills necessary to move to the next level is going to make mistakes and possibly endanger lives.

The question is often asked why Willie was 'only' a corporal at 35. There are two reasons. One, he came from the Territorials and only became a full-time SAS member in 2002. He hadn't had the opportunities for advancement that come in the Regular Army. Two, he's been quite busy. Moreover, in many ways, to think of rank at all is counter to the SAS egalitarian ethos, with its first names and no saluting. It isn't something unit members pursue with much vigour.

There is also some arithmetic involved. The SAS does not quite advance people on a 'dead man's shoes' principle, but it does have a limit on the number of people it can have at each rank.

In the long-term, many years are left to Willie in the SAS – and it is not an organisation one grows old in. He can expect more opportunities rather than fewer as a result of his VC. Things have been managed so – and his personality is such that – he won't end up hanging off the end of a bottle as have some others. He hasn't reached the halfway point in the fame cycle yet, but inevitably, and to his and the SAS's relief, curiosity about him will wane.

But what he personifies will remain, and he will always be thought of, and his example brought up, when certain qualities are debated. Whatever else happens in his future, his combination of energy and old-fashioned values is likely to continue to inspire others. He represents a New Zealand spirit that many thought had ceased production some time ago: a combination of common sense, non-materialism – he is one of the few people who are believable when they say they don't care about possessions – closeness to nature, self-sufficiency, and living in the present, which is a key to his philosophy.

There's a picture on a packet of smokes with a ruined set of lungs and a fresh set. But the fresh set is taken from a dead guy. What's the point of having a clean set of lungs if you're dead? The fresh set could have been run over by a truck at 18, the other set could be from an 80-year-old. That's why you have to live your life to the full every day.

I get a lot of satisfaction out of hunting, even if I don't catch anything; the bush is a place to go and think. If you catch something, you're filling up your family's freezer. I'm the man of our family and I want to look after my whanau. The bush was always our larder.

I've always appreciated what little we had and I always will. Money means a lot more in town because it's the only way you can survive in the city. Street kids in town go through rubbish bins or burgle houses to survive. Their goal is committing crimes to live. They have to. Down home, in the country, you don't have to. The only reason you wouldn't survive would be if you were lazy.

I am in a job that I enjoy. I have my share of bad days, but all it takes is a little bit of a rest and maybe unloading on somebody and you will either fix it or crack on and get over it.

I've had more good things happen to me in life than bad things. There's got to be some hard times. A friend once told me that sugar cane has two ends, a sweet end and a sour end. You should start at the sour end first, work hard and eventually you will get to the sweet end.

Willie may not see himself as any kind of public speaker, or any sort of hero, beyond being Willie Apiata, but he is always happy to spend time with young people. Among his troop of nieces and nephews he is adored, not just for the fact he has a Victoria Cross, but because he is always willing to give them time – to show them how to handle a horse, how to hunt or catch eels, or merely play backyard dodge ball with them or conduct an informal investiture ceremony at The Land in which everyone gets a medal.

Just as the VC has not changed Willie's place in the family, it also hasn't altered how that next generation regards him. They have been almost as unspoilt by the event as he has. When Willie visited one of their schools at the whanau's request, a teacher asked the class: 'What does Willie mean to you?'

For most of the kids the answers involved war, guns and a Victoria Cross. For Willie's whanau the answer was: 'He's our uncle.'

'Anything else?'

'He brings us presents.'

Willie is always firm in pointing out that his job is not about war and death, but about life and the years ahead. After his time with the SAS, his sights are most firmly fixed on his son. That is where his long-term focus lies.

At my investiture you could hear him saying 'Dad'. Someone asked me if it was a proud moment when he said that, and I said it's a proud moment every time he calls me Dad.

I missed out on so much when he was young: starting to crawl and talk and walk. All those things happened without me there, because of my job. Now he's of an age where, when I go away, I'll be able to explain to him what's happening and he will understand. And he won't have forgotten me by the time I get back and have to learn who I am all over again.

I don't expect anything of him except to behave and listen to the old man and respect his elders. He is a lot like me. He's quite big for his age, he loves the outdoors, and he's a bolt of energy, from the moment his eyes are open till they close. He loves hunting, he loves riding horses and camping and playing with the fire and all that sort of stuff. He is five and he's not afraid when I shoot an animal. The only thing that made him a little bit sick the first time I took him is when I started cutting up the guts.

'Don't look, look over there,' I said.

'No, I want to look.'

He wants to learn. When I first stuck him on the horse when he was four, he screamed. An old farmer was there saying, 'Is he going to be okay? Has he been on a horse before?' I said, 'No, first time.'

I had him sitting in front of me, and we had our packhorse at the back with our gear on it and we started riding down the road with him screaming. But by the time we got to Raukokore Bridge, the screaming had subsided and he was sniffling.

'You all right, boy?'

'Yeah, yeah, yeah. This is a nice horse, eh, Dad?'

'Yeah, it is, boy. You all right?'

'Yeah, I'm okay now,' he says, and after half an hour riding up the river I put him on the back of the packhorse and he was right as rain. I'd either lead it with my hand or tie it to the tail of the other horse and let it follow.

He stayed on the horse on a lot of tracks where even I get off because they're always boggy. The cowboy saddle gives him something to hold on to. And he loves it.

We stayed up there for two nights. I told him: 'We don't do toiletries up there. There's no brushing your teeth every night and morning, and we wear the same clothes until we get out.' The only thing I take up is pyjamas so that when he goes to sleep he can take off all his dirty clothes, jump in his bag and feel good.

He loves bugs. In the bush I've opened up big logs and shown him the huhu grubs in there. He's not frightened of them. And he has respect for bees and wasps because he's been stung. He's not frightened of them either. I'll teach him as much as I can about being self-sufficient.

I'm trying to prepare him, because when I go, he'll be taking my place. I don't expect him to join the Army and follow in my footsteps, but I want him to be able to make a choice. I'd rather him choose something that he really wants to do than just end up doing something to pay the bills.

Before he's finished growing up I'd like to have settled down back in Te Kaha. There's a piece of land there I have my eye on, near where I go hunting all the time. I know I'll be able to accomplish anything else I want to do in life from there, even though it's remote. There is some cellphone coverage, but you get to a point where there's just a big black spot, and that's where I want to be – right on the black spot.

That's the sort of environment where I'd like to finish raising my young fella. There will come a day when it will happen. I'm not destined to leave the SAS yet, but when I am, I will know the time is right.

I'll do what I've always wanted to do, which is breaking horses, going hunting with my boy and handing over a bit of the knowledge that I have been given.

THE TEST

It was the start of winter, nearly a year after I got the VC, and it took so many weeks for the river back home to go down. I couldn't get up it for the first month, so I looked around and came in the back, which is a hua of a journey, but I ended up only going halfway, because as I was about to cross over the saddle and drop into the valley I came across a hind and shot it.

I turned around and went down another stream. It was an amazing journey. I walked down a gorge with my pack on and my deer over the top of it. There were places where I was paddling and the stream was only as wide as a car. There was rock all the way up on either side. There was only one place where I couldn't get down in the water and had to climb up through the bush, bypass it and come back down into the stream.

At one point I had to put the deer on a rock and position it so that once

I'd jumped into the water I would be able to reach up, grab its leg and get down. I couldn't tell from looking at it how deep the water was because it was so crystal clear.

When I jumped in, it was right up to my neck. I was reaching up and could just tickle the ends of the hoofs. I managed to pull it enough to get it down and catch it on my pack and start paddling. I always trap a bit of air in my backpack, so that when I'm cruising in the water I float. When I've got a deer on, the air compensates for the weight. I've come out of a flooded river with a pig on my back like that.

I go up there every year with my backpack. For me, it's my test before I come back to work. When I can no longer carry animals out of the bush, maybe then it will be time to move on into the office.

NEW ZEALAND VICTORIA CROSS WINNERS

Corporal Leslie Wilton Andrew; 2nd Wellington Regt., 1st NZEF; 31 July 1917; Basseville, France; 6 September 1917. He later joined the N.Z. Staff Corps, rising to the rank of brigadier, and was awarded the D.S.O. during the Second World War.

Corporal Bill Henry Apiata; 1 NZSAS Group; 2 July 2007; Afghanistan. This is the first VC for New Zealand.

Corporal Cyril Royston Guyton Bassett; N.Z. Divisional Signal Coy., 1st NZEF; 7 August 1915; Chunuk Bair Ridge, Gallipoli; 15 October 1915. This was the first New Zealand award during the First World War.

Sergeant Donald Forrester Brown; 2nd Battalion, N.Z. Infantry, 1st NZEF; 15 September 1916; south-east of High Wood, France; 14 June 1917. (Posthumous award.)

Private James Crichton; 2nd Battalion, Auckland Regt., 1st NZEF; 30 September 1918; Crevecoeur, France; 15 November 1918. Died at Auckland on 22 September 1961, aged 82 years.

Sergeant Keith Elliott; 22nd Battalion, 2nd NZEF; 15 July 1942, Ruweisat, Western Desert; 24 September 1942. Became a clerk in holy orders after the war.

Sergeant Samuel Forsyth; N.Z. Engineers attached 2nd Auckland Battalion, 1st NZEF; 24 August 1918; Grevillers, France; 22 October 1918. (Posthumous award.)

Lance-Corporal Samuel Frickleton; 3rd Battalion, N.Z. Rifle Brigade, 1st NZEF; 7 July 1917; Messines, Belgium; 2 August 1918.

Sergeant John Gilroy Grant; 1st Battalion, Wellington Regt., 1st NZEF; 1 September 1918; near Bancourt, France; 27 November 1918.

Farrier-Major William James Hardham; 4th Contingent, N.Z. Mounted Rifles; 28 January 1901; near Naauwpoort, South Africa; 4 October 1901. Later a major, he died on 13 April 1928.

Captain Charles Heaphy; Auckland Militia; 11 February 1864; Mangapiko River, New Zealand; 8 February 1867. Later a major, he died at Brisbane, Australia, on 3 August 1881, aged 59 years.

Sergeant John Daniel Hinton; 20th Battalion, 2nd NZEF; 28–29 April 1941; Kalamai, Greece; 17 October 1941.

Sergeant Alfred Clive Hulme; 23rd Battalion, 2nd NZEF; 20–28 May 1941; Maleme, Galatos, Suda Bay, and Stylos, Crete; 14 October 1941.

Sergeant Reginald Stanley Judson, D.C.M., M.M.; 1st Battalion, Auckland Regt., 1st NZEF; 26 August 1918; south of Bapaume, France; 30 October 1918.

Sergeant Harry John Laurent; 2nd Battalion, N.Z. Rifle Brigade, 1st NZEF; 12 September 1918; east of Gouzeaucourt Wood, France; 15 November 1918.

Second-Lieutenant Moananui-a-Kiwa Ngarimu; 28th (Maori) Battalion, 2nd NZEF; 26 March 1943; Tebaga Gap, Tunisia; 4 June 1943. (Posthumous award.)

Private Henry James Nicholas; 1st Battalion, Canterbury Regt., 1st NZEF; 3 December 1917; Polderhoek, Belgium; 11 January 1918.

Sergeant Richard Charles Travis, D.C.M., M.M.; 2nd Battalion Otago Regt., 1st NZEF; 24 July 1918; north of Hebuterne, France; 27 September 1918. (Posthumous award.) His correct name was Dickson Cornelius Savage, but he enlisted and served under the family name of Travis.

Squadron Leader Leonard Henry Trent, D.F.C.; RNZAF (No. 487 (N.Z.) Sqn. RAF); 3 May 1943; over Amsterdam, Holland; 1 March 1946.

Flying Officer Lloyd Allan Trigg, D.F.C.; RNZAF (No. 200 Sqn. RAF); 11 August 1943; anti-submarine patrol, Atlantic Ocean; 2 November 1943. (Posthumous award.)

Second-Lieutenant Charles Hazlitt Upham; 20th Battalion, 2nd NZEF. V.C. –22–30 May 1941; Maleme, Galatos, and Sphakia, Crete; 14 October 1941. Bar – As a captain; 14 July 1942; Ruweisat Ridge, Western Desert; 26 September 1945.

Sergeant-Pilot James Allen Ward; RNZAF (No. 75 (N.Z.) Sqn. RAF); 7 July 1941; over the Zuider Zee, Holland; 5 August 1941. This was the first New Zealand award during the Second World War. He was killed on operations over Germany on 15 September 1941.

Source: www.teara.govt.nz